FAITH, STRENGTH, AND COURAGE

A Memoir of Overcoming Adversity & Embracing Life's Journey.

by Gregory O. Proctor

Gregory O. Proctor

Acknowledgment

To my dearest Monica,

As I sit down to write these words, my heart overflows with love and gratitude for you. This book is not just a testament to my journey but also a tribute to the love and support you have showered upon me these past two years.

When I was first diagnosed with multiple myeloma, our world was turned upside down. The uncertainty, fear, and challenges that lay ahead seemed insurmountable. But through it all, you became my rock, my guiding light, and my source of unwavering strength.

Your love, Monica, was the anchor that grounded me in the face of adversity. Your presence is a constant reminder I was never alone in this battle. Through every doctor's appointment, chemo session, and sleepless night, you stood by my side, offering me solace. Your unconditional love was my sanctuary, providing comfort and reassurance in my darkest moments. Your unwavering support gave me the courage to face each day with renewed hope and determination. Without you, I honestly don't know how I would have survived this challenging journey.

In the pages of this book, I have poured out my heart, sharing the raw emotions and the profound lessons I learned along the way. But I could not have learned them without your unwavering belief in me.

You have shown me the true meaning of love, and I am forever grateful to have you as my partner. As this book finds its way into the hands of readers, I want the world to know that behind my every word, triumph, and moment of growth, there is a woman whose love has been the foundation upon which my life has been rebuilt.

Thank you, Mi Amor, for your support, love, and unwavering belief in me. You are my heart's home, and I am eternally grateful for the gift of your presence in my life. I love you, Monica, always and forever. Your loving husband, Gregory

In addition, my deepest gratitude goes to my family:

Jessie Proctor, Regina Aldana, Victoria Proctor, Rosa Aldana, Gabriela Proctor, Jason Proctor, Miluska Coello Aldana, Shonda Allen Hill, Ph.D., Claudia P. Coello Aldana, Voretta Allen Nesby, Paola Coello Aldana, Vida Williams, Luciana Coello Aldana, JP Allen, Alfredo Melly, Manuel A. Coello Garcia, and Aldo Escalante.

My dearest friends:

Jacqueline Smith, Robert Marshall, Kalee Nixon, Tony Fuentes, Will Sims, Sylvester Jenkins, Greg Brisco, Tanjia Coleman, Ph.D., Julie Hruska, Peggy Burkhard, Robert Allen, Brenda Chavers, TiJa Mitchell Sr., Eunice Ifeanyichukwu, John Moreno, Patricia Zich Hoyhtya, Lizette Figueroa, and Bobby Dee Hervey.

The medical practitioners who fought tirelessly to save me:

Dr. Sudhir R. Gogu, Dr. Micheal S. McKee, Dr. Jayasree Rao, Laura Rodriguez, Shay Tso, Ann Ross, Cynthia Hernandez, Patricia Mendez, Christie Alvarado Lucio, Fanny Juarez, Dr. David Haile, Dr. Chung, Dr. Dacus, Dr. Irene Ghobrial, and Dr. Monique A. Hartley-Brown.

My friends and followers on Facebook, LinkedIn, and Kuth2thaChase.

And Dolores Allen Paige, Supt. Unice C. Brazil and Rickey Chavers, who are sadly no longer with us.

Thank you so much. This book has been a labor of love fueled by the encouragement and belief you have always shown me. Your presence in my life, your comments, and your support gave me the confidence to share my story with the world, and I am eternally grateful for that.

Thank you for believing in me and for reminding me of the power of love and friendship. I wouldn't have this or be here without you.

With deepest gratitude,

Gregory

Table of Contents

Gregory O. Proctor

Foreword

by Shonda Allen Hill, Ph.D.

There are great stories and epic novels, but this seminal work of Gregory Proctor (affectionately called Greg) stands in a category of its own. Combining the grit of life's conflicts and the grace of growth, healing, and freedom, Greg introduces the literary world to a new concept of strength—one of being vulnerable, demanding, empathetic, and powerful—all in a single interaction.

I have known Greg my entire life. Or at least I thought I did. Born in the once-sleepy, now sprawling town of Brandon, Mississippi, Greg could easily pass for the typical "boy next door." We were cousins. Dirt-kicking, ball throwing, snack-eating first cousins. So close that the academic rules of parenting, including discipline, flowed freely from one set of parents to the next without an explanation of detail or a question regarding any action. Our family ties, the blood that binds us, run deep. Yet, with every passing year, it was clear that Greg operates on a higher plain.

Greg is not just different; he embodies different. The kind of different that fuels the world. It is his kryptonite and his superpower.

In his early years, I thought I knew him as a child. A precocious, gritty, playful child. But I soon realized that he was, then, the early embodiment of today's version of a boss baby.

As an adolescent, I thought I knew him as a card-trading, comic-book-collecting, emerging track extraordinaire. One who would follow a traditional path to reach the American Dream. However, I soon realized that his passion for his country and his drive to break corporate barriers required him to blaze uncharted paths and soar over unfamiliar territories.

Today, as a man of honor and strength, I thought I knew him as an accomplished adult who loves his family and supports his friends.

But after watching him battle and survive multiple myeloma, I've realized that he's a hell fighter, a stormtrooper, a crusading warrior.

Greg's memoir speaks loudly of the pain of regret, the disappointment of detoured dreams, and the horror of living in the balance between life and death. But what speaks loudest is the heartbeat of hope that is resounding through this work: Faith, Strength, and Courage.

This book is a sigh of relief to the weary, a breath of fresh air to the broken, and a healing strength to the hurting.

A new day is here. A new warrior, Gregory O. Proctor, is born.

Chaos and Things Unfulfilled

It was surreal the way my father died. It was surreal and heartbreaking.

My mother had called me weeks earlier, her voice low and sober. "I need you to come home," she said. "Your father is in the hospital." It felt strange that she suddenly needed me there. My father had been sick for years, sick enough that he needed care but not so sick we were scared he would die soon. And my mother, she had handled his care with frightening independence, the way she'd done everything her whole life.

So, as I listened to her voice that day with my elbow resting on my desk covered with piles of ongoing projects, I knew this call was different.

With a feeling of foreboding, I packed my bags two days later and drove fourteen hours from Virginia straight to the hospital in Mississippi, knowing I wouldn't return the same. It had been hard to abandon my work, to give up even for a day, the thing that drove me and gave me an anxious sense of purpose. So I packed my work phone and laptop, too, because I didn't want to be unreachable. And because I hoped I was mistaken, and my mother's voice was not as low as I'd heard. If it wasn't, I could sneak in some hours of work when she wasn't looking.

But the minute I got to the hospital and saw her standing at the entrance with her hands wrapped around her body like she was trying to keep warm, I knew she had understated. Her sadness was palpable. It permeated the air, filling up the space between us and making me involuntarily gasp for air as I hugged her.

"I think it's time," she said.

And I knew enough not to say anything back, enough to immediately understand my father was dying. Trying and failing to quell the panic rising in my throat, I followed her as she walked into the hospital.

When we arrived at the door to my father's room, a group of doctors pulled me aside and, with just the right mixture of aloofness and sobriety, said, "We are so sorry, Mr. Proctor. Your father's organs are shutting down. There's nothing else we can do. His body has run its course. We need to pull the plug."

A few years back, my mother had relinquished all control to me for this very purpose, but I'd hoped it would never come to this. So I stood there completely blindsided like someone had thrown me abruptly into an impromptu debate and was expecting me to win. The doctors stood there patiently waiting for me to say something, and I took several deep breaths to calm myself. I made them wait a little longer, perhaps longer than they cared for, because yes, this was routine for them, and perhaps they would stop in the next room to deliver similar news to another family, but this was monumental for me. I was about to lose my father, a man who had been something of a stern stranger to me for most of my life, and I needed to catch my breath.

Moments later, I walked into my father's room and stood looking at him as he slept, his breathing aided by the soft whirring of mechanical ventilation. He'd always seemed so big to me, in the way fathers seem like giants to their kids, but that image had remained for me even as an adult—even when I resented him for being the absent father who couldn't make it to my track races or school functions. But here he was, suddenly small and human, looking frail. I fought back my tears then. I fought them as I sat next to him and told him, though he couldn't hear me, that we had to pull the plug.

"It's okay, son," my mother said, suddenly standing next to me and clutching my hands. "It's okay."

Everything ceased for me then. Nothing else mattered. It did not work, and not the adrenaline from it that sent my heart racing. I sat by his side every day for twenty days, talking to him even though he couldn't hear or talk back and listening to the many stories of visitors who came to see him and pay their last respects.

These visitors painted an image of my father I'd never seen before. Their stories were those of a stranger, a father I'd never met. They spoke of his kindness and compassion, his empathy and warmth.

"Your father was a good man," an old friend of his said. "The best. He would give you the clothes off his back. I never met someone who sacrificed more for what he believed in and the people he loved."

"He spoke of you a lot," the man said, and I stared at him, speechless. "He was very proud."

Those twenty-one days of listening to friends and colleagues talk about how empathetic and warm my dad was brought things full circle for me. It felt like I was meeting my father for the first time. I'd always thought of my dad as a hard man. And he was, to me and my younger siblings. But hearing these stories about him gave me a sense of pride and validation. It made me love him more. I'd never experienced this side of him. It was great to know he'd always had it.

Though I was ready for it, his death hit me like a mighty, crashing wave. I choked back tears as the doctor pulled the plug. And afterward, knowing he was gone, I still felt his palm for a pulse, movement, anything. I willed him to come back so I could meet the man his friends had talked so lovingly about. It felt like I was losing my father, just as I'd found him.

His death had seemed surreal, like a movie, because before then, I hadn't thought about death. So, to find it in my father's face was daunting. Because of him, death became a living, breathing thing in my mind, accompanied by grief that left me unsteady. So I downed this unwanted reality with tall glasses of denial, throwing myself back into work with a vengeance, allowing my work days to run into nights and my nights into days; days that stretched and stretched and created exhaustion that was bone deep. I piled my to-do list with more than I could do in a day, creating projects when I ran out, traveling two-hundred thousand miles a year, and working fourteen hours a day and seven days a week. Fourteen-hour days that often stretched into twenty on the days I couldn't bring myself to stop. Work had always been the place I could go, like it had been for my father. And though I had resented him for it, it was the one thing about him I took and made mine. In his absence, work reminded me of him and became a comfort—a twisted, unfulfilling comfort.

I looked forward to it every day, creating elaborate to-do lists, ticking things off, and adding even more. Until one day, years later, life erased everything on my list and replaced it with one word—survive.

Though I would get diagnosed in July, the first pain hit my back several months earlier in May, almost a year after the onset of COVID-19. It came randomly as if someone had tentatively taken a hammer to my back, pounding to see how I would react. But I didn't react. Except for the occasional cold, I had never been sick a day in my life, so this back pain felt like the result of one too many fourteen-hour days. Also, it was a work day, a Tuesday. I was working and, like most people in the world whose mental health had been teetering on the edge for a year, avoiding the news.

As if on the orders of a vengeful God, COVID had swept through the world, leaving chaos and heartbreak in its wake. Systems and morals disintegrated, with people climbing on top of each other to survive while the medical community scurried around to find a cure. I watched this chaos in horror and heartbreak but also with disgust and ire. The disease had brought our lives and livelihoods to a standstill, and my business had taken a hit.

I worked as a Projects Controls and Management Consultant for ten years. I did long before my father died. My job included providing consultancy services for the government and commercialized industries, and I'd become a master at it. My mastery was so good it led colleagues, partners, and employees alike to call me "brilliant" and "asshole" in the same breath.

But I didn't care. If anything, I thrived on this divided view of me because it brought me the best contracts and gave me seats at the most influential and expensive tables in corporate America.

Being Black American in a sea of white colleagues and competition was aggravating. I would walk into client meetings and have conversations pause in surprise, disbelief, anger, or disgust. And if I stayed long enough in the meetings, I was demeaned, disrespected, or dismissed. It didn't matter that I'd left a trail of successful projects in my wake or that I came highly recommended; the color of my skin was always the disqualification. One time, though I'd been recommended and introduced by a powerful white client, the moment the potential white client saw me, he refused to work with me.

To combat this prejudice, I had to wear an air of aloofness and sternness, combined with an arrogance that let them know I would not be disrespected on the basis of my skin or anything else for that matter. I had no patience for white baby boomers who looked down on me or black colleagues who didn't try to fight back. I was a small fish in a big and hostile pond, smack in the middle of the biggest opportunities in some of the biggest companies in the world. In the end, I sat at those expensive and influential tables because I clawed and fought my way in. I had to have enough notion and persistence in my life to go up against racism and prejudice, and that earned me the "asshole" nickname.

In 2018, I started my own project controls and management consultancy firm, SchXer. Two years later, when COVID hit, I was on the road a lot with my team, rounding up on some government projects. We were finishing up projects and were on the verge of signing contracts for new ones when whispers of an unknown virus began circling the ranks. In my driven and self-centered world, the emergence of this new virus would not have mattered to me, except its widespread and dire nature began to attack an essential part of my business: mobility.

Being a Projects Controls and Management Consultant meant that we did a lot of strategic-development planning, risk analysis, cost estimation, oversight, and supervision. It also meant stepping into disarray and creating order. We were always hired in the thick of it amidst the chaos of sometimes bumbling clients who'd waited until the last minute to call because they thought they knew what they were doing.

They often had similar issues: they had gone over budget, were behind schedule, or just had no idea what direction the project was going. So they needed an intervention, a fixer, a correction factor, and that was me. I would get in there feeling like Jesus in the middle of the storm, waving his hands to calm the sea while his disciples cowered in fear. Except unlike Jesus, I was arrogant and obnoxious, and fixing things sometimes meant I had to unintentionally and intentionally break the will of others.

I did all of that while securing billions of dollars in revenue for these companies and making lucrative earnings for myself. However, the significant aspect of this was I had to do this work in person. That was never an issue for me because being on the road so much, even though it had aggravated my ex-wife and two daughters, was a part of the job I loved. But COVID stole that from me, and I had to explain to clients I had worked with for years that I could calm their storms remotely.

Baby boomers, the majority of my clientele, had looked at me aghast. "Remotely?" they echoed in disbelief.

"Yes, remotely," I replied over video calls. "Of course, being physically there has its benefits, but the majority of the work can be done remotely."

"Do we still have to pay you the same compensation?"

"Well, yes," I said, trying to control my patience. "I'd still be doing the work."

"We will have to get back to you on that, Greg," they said, with every intention of not getting back to me.

After the fifth similar call, I signed off and massaged my temples. Eventually, in my aggravation, I realized that more than COVID, I was furious with these baby boomers—these clients who now, after years of partnership and hard work, wanted me to prove my worth and experience all over again. Their lack of trust and constant rigmarole angered me. I thought I had built a community of people, a circle of contacts who could trust my work without me physically there to oversee it. I had given my hours and skills, missed birthdays and anniversaries, risked my health many times to get them what they needed, and they couldn't walk through the inconvenience of COVID with me. My frustration grew with the death toll numbers until, for the first time in my life, I paused and took a step back.

It occurred to me then that this was no longer fun. It hadn't been for years. I was driven, not purposeful; I was unfulfilled. The weight of this realization sent me into a tailspin, and I found myself seeking for things and people to make me whole.

COVID had stopped the world on its axis, making me realize I hadn't been moving all this time.

Forced to have time on my hands or rather less work, I searched for a new thing. The death toll numbers climbed, and I searched for a new thing. The images of rows and rows of coffins filled our TV screens, coffins designated for mass burials, the dead sent off without the simple privilege of their loved ones crying over their coffins, and I searched for a new thing. The COVID year drew to an end, and still, I searched for a new thing.

I had never gone a day in my life unoccupied, even as a child. Having to do that now terrified me, so I wasn't going to take a break simply because the world demanded it.

The new year began, and I sorted out projects as the first pain hit my back. I ignored the pain as it climbed and searched even harder. Ignoring the pounding as it got bolder was easy because it appeared with an irregularity that made me brush it aside.

I helped friends and colleagues with projects and worked on creating something new for myself—determined to keep myself working while COVID, almost a year later, still unbelievably raged.

Working was my way of raging right back, of reminding myself there was light at the end of this very bleak tunnel.

It was in this state I created the thing that gave me purpose, only to turn around and ignore it for the thing that drained me.

The week everything changed, I woke up to a searing pain in my back, pushing down aggressively to my hip bone. It was a defining pain, one that left me scared and made me realize it had been building up more rapidly than I'd noticed.

It's that damn chair, I thought, as I rolled over to my current wife's side of the bed. Unable to travel, I was spending my days immobile in my chair, working. I still had many personal projects, so I was just as busy as I had been before COVID.

The emptiness of my wife's side of the bed made me groan even louder. My current wife, Monica (I affectionately called her Mi Amor), whom I'd been married to for five years, had been commuting back and forth from Peru since the beginning of COVID to take care of her family, and I missed her terribly. I texted her quickly to let her know I was up, smiling pleasantly at the messages we had exchanged the night before. It was hard being without her during this period, but no one knew how to keep in touch better than she did.

Doing my best to manage the pain, I got up, brushed, and jumped in the shower with thoughts of my work for the day circling my head. I had three meetings: a podcast to edit, a discovery call to get on, an investor meeting for Tru-Spot, another investor meeting to pitch Tru-spot, and yet another social media post to edit for Tru-Spot. Sighing, I got out and dried myself. Everything on the list sounded demanding and exhausting, everything except the podcast.

I thought about skipping breakfast, but the pain intensified, and I made my way to the kitchen to make toast. Monica made the most delicious meals when she was home, and biting into my dry toast made me miss her even more. Done; I washed it down with some lemon juice and grabbed some Tylenol from the kitchen pantry cabinet. I popped two pills, dropped the container back in the cabinet, walked out, and came back a second later to take it. I thought of drugs as a necessity, something you took only when you absolutely had to. The pain in my back insisted I needed the pills, so I took them and walked to my work desk.

As I neared it, an involuntary groan escaped my lips at the sight of my workspace, and it surprised me. The extrovert in me hated being confined to a space, hated that the option of going wherever I wanted, whenever I wanted, had been taken away from me. Somehow, this workspace represented all COVID had stolen from me. Still, I could go for a walk whenever I wanted to, yet I spent all my time confined in my work space—much to Monica's vexation.

Sighing, I took my seat and cracked my knuckles. Another pain shot through my back, and I wrote a new task on my to-do list: get rid of this damn chair. Somewhat satisfied, I dove into my first task of the day—editing the video for our Tru-Spot channel on YouTube. We had an interactive new mobile app coming out, and I wanted to explain to our potential users how to navigate it.

Tru-Spot was the brainchild of Will Sims, my oldest friend. We reconnected three years ago. We grew up together as childhood friends but lost contact over the years, with me going into project management and consultancy and him going into Human Resources. But our mothers had stayed devoted friends, and that had been enough to reconnect.

When Will brought Tru-Spot to me three years ago, I was at the height of my consultancy business. I didn't have time to take on any side projects, and my honor of his request had been more of an indulgence. He was more than a friend: I thought of him as a brother, and I was not going to say no to him. He wanted me to come on as a consultant, and I agreed—until I took a closer look at Tru-Spot and convinced him we could make it so much more.

Will wanted to create an interactive experience for football fans to heighten their appreciation and love of the sport. But I convinced him we could upgrade it into augmented reality for fan engagement.

We met over lunch so he could explain the design to me, and after genuine pleasantries, he got right to business.

"How do we remove the chains in American football?" he asked cryptically.

"Chains?" I asked, puzzled.

"Yes. How do we remove the chains and have a digitized way of measuring the ball every time it goes down the yard."

"Well," I said, impressed.

He laughed. "I knew you would like the idea."

I did. I had come here to see the man I considered to be my big brother, to catch up and indulge his big ideas along the way. But what he said interested me more than I anticipated, and the more he talked, the more I realized I wanted to be more than a consultant.

He talked some more about his vision for the app, and each reveal heightened my interest. When he was done, I was fully convinced.

"I want to be a partner."

"You mean that?" he asked in delighted surprise.

I nodded. "But if I come on, you have to fire the Indian software development company you hired. They don't know what they are doing. Fire them. Let me research and find us the best way to disrupt the tech world."

He burst into joyous laughter and clapped my back heartily, nearly spilling my drink. "I knew I was right to bring you on!" he said.

And so it began. I got on board, and we began to discuss ideas.

"What if we put a chip in the ball?" I said one time, and he nodded in excitement.

"We could enhance our augmented reality even more," I said another time, and he agreed. I could see he trusted my judgment, and that made me even bolder. But even as I dropped idea after idea, I realized Tru-Spot was missing something I couldn't quite put my finger on.

Until a week later, to Monica's alarm, I ran out of the shower to call Will.

"Will!" I yelled when he picked up. "I've got it! What if we give the user an augmented reality that gives them a 360 view of the stadium?!"

"What?" he said.

"Imagine this," I said. "I'm in San Antonio right now, and you could be in Washington or Africa or anywhere in the world, but we'd both be able to sit side by side in the stadium, go up and down the stairs, or left and right, and watch the game as if we are both physically there at the same time!"

"WOW!"

"I know! And we could have this software available on any device. They could use it from the comfort of their homes, office, car, anywhere!"

Will was floored and excited, and when the full realization of my idea hit me, so was I. We were doing something revolutionary, and though we didn't know it yet, in three years, COVID would make the world desperate for a connection like this. This idea cemented my partnership with Will, but it also made it disproportionate. I carried the burden of creativity and execution of Tru-Spot while Will sourced for investors.

Will didn't know much about technology. His idea was one he had nursed since he was in high school, something his soul yearned to create. The more we worked together, the more I realized why. He had that unfulfilled need to create something that was unequivocally his. I understood it.

But even with the genius of Tru-Spot and the excited buzz we got from the tech community, getting it off the ground was a challenge, and securing investors for it was hell.

Getting buzz for Tru-Spot wasn't as hard as we anticipated; in fact, it was the easy part. Every tech writer and magazine wanted to interview us, and they did, over and over. We appeared in articles and magazines, each one detailing the wonder of Tru-Spot and all the possibilities it could accomplish for the sports world. We had celebrity and nationwide recognition. But all of that publicity couldn't get us the thing we desperately needed: investors.

Confident in the viability and possibilities of our app, we were selective with investors at first. But after we got increasingly rejected, we began to send out pitch after pitch to every investor we could find. Many of them were impressed with our app, but as if reading from a rehearsed line, all of them said the same thing, "You are too early to the market."

They weren't wrong. We were early to the market, but we had to be. Being early to the market was the only way to get publicity, and publicity meant investors, and investors meant funding, and funding meant we could finish the app and get it to market. The investors wanted the app to be ready before they invested, but the app couldn't be ready without their money. Explaining this to them felt like going around in a circle, and we did, for months—to the point whenever Will came to me with another investor, I groaned internally. Suddenly, what seemed like a revolutionary idea felt like an exhausting, tiring cycle. Also, some of the investors didn't like that we were Black. There's a reason there are very few tech start-ups headed by Black founders. I'd worked enough in corporate America to know that lack of representation and prejudiced investors were just some of the reasons. The glaring lack of diversity in venture capital firms, racial discrimination, funding gaps, and lack of social capital preceded us. We were just one in thousands of Black start-ups denied investments and recognition simply because we weren't white.

However, their refusal to fund the app only spurred us on. We pooled our savings and worked tirelessly to bring the app to life. My personal projects began to suffer, our savings began to dwindle, and Monica was not impressed.

"You are letting Tru-Spot consume you," she said. "You need to take a step back."

"It will all be worth it soon," I would say. "We are working on another investor. Soon, Mi Amor."

And she would walk away, shaking her head.

But I had no idea how soon it would be, and I wasn't certain I could take a step back on my own. Tru-Spot had become an obsession, a need, a challenge that I just had to conquer. Somewhere along the line, it had stopped being about Will or connecting people to their loved ones during an exciting game and more about the rush, the adrenaline I got from creating something so utterly brand new and unheard of. I wanted the satisfaction of saying, "Look, I made this!" I wanted to leave something behind.

My involvement became about my ego. I wanted to do something that would get me admitted into any room by anyone. But it also became about being Black, about the prejudice and discrimination I'd suffered. I'd been looked over my whole life and talked down to because of the color of my skin, and creating something like Tru-Spot would finally change that, or at least drastically reduce it. I wanted my accomplishment to precede me. Even if they hated me for the color of my skin, they had to accept me and need me for what I'd done.

I never got this rush from my project controls and management consultancy business. I had gotten so used to fixing their chaos that it had become boring and repetitive. I could do it seamlessly now, so much so that some days when I woke up, it felt like I was waking up to yesterday. Even before COVID and the fast exodus of my clients, my days had blended into one, and I couldn't tell them apart anymore until Tru-Spot.

Two hours later, as I put the finishing touches to the YouTube video, I wondered if Will had found another investor yet, and I cringed at the thought. I didn't have the energy to tell them why we were early to the market again.

My reminder for my meeting with Will went off. I turned it off, stretched my back, and felt a searing pain shoot downward to my hips. What in the hell? I cursed as I hurriedly opened the cap of the Tylenol container and popped two pills into my mouth. I stood for a while, waiting for the pain to subside. It didn't, and I groaned harder. I could feel the pain in my hips. It was steady and throbbing. You need to get rid of this damn chair, I thought as I stretched. And go for a damn walk! Monica would be upset if she found out I'd spent that long on a chair without moving. She had been begging me to get up and go for a walk for weeks. I planned to, but I was just too busy.

Trying to shake off the pain, I signed into our video call and waited for Will to show up. Five minutes later, he hadn't, and I shook my head in surprise. Will was never late. My phone rang, and I glanced at it. It was Will. I picked it up.

"Will," I started, "don't we have…?"

His voice reverberated with excitement. "We got it!" he yelled. "We got into Mass Challenge!"

Speechless, I held the phone to my ear. "I'm sorry, Will," I said after a moment. "I thought I heard you say we got into Mass Challenge."

"Yes! I'm staring at the email right now."

"Oh, my God," I said softly, unable to say anything else. "Oh, my God."

"I know!" Will said, laughing joyously. "It's finally happening!"

That was an understatement. This was three years of long and sleepless nights, of putting my business on hold, of getting into fights with my wife because I was spending too much time and money on this and not enough time on our livelihood, of canceling plans and forgetting birthdays. Three years of writing extensive and elaborate pitches that got denied, rejected, and laughed at. Of meetings with investors who hid their disdain and racism very poorly. Of fearing that the longer we waited to get funding, the sooner our idea would become redundant. Of being told to give up because there was no way we would succeed anyway; we were just two Veterans from Mississippi—what were the odds?

Will had quit his job, sold his house, and sunk his savings into this to make it happen. It was a bigger dream for him than it was for me, and I shuddered to think what would happen if we hadn't gotten in. My mind began to spin; there was now even more to do. I felt a wave of exhaustion hit me, but I reined it in. This was not the time to get tired. There were press conferences to hold, social media campaigns to handle, and meetings to schedule and unschedule—all of these would fall into my lap because Will had no idea about this side of the business.

"So, what do we do next?" I asked, already going through my calendar to see what I needed to schedule, cancel, or move.

"I'll call you back in an hour so we can properly go over that. Let me forward the email to you."

"Alright," I said, and then quickly glanced at my to-do list. "No. I have a discovery meeting with a government client after this, another meeting with one of my contractors, and a discovery meeting for my podcast episode." I sighed. "But that's okay; I can move that last one."

"Well, good, because we have pitches to write."

My excitement dwindled. "We have to write more pitches?" I had written more pitches than I cared for.

"Yes," Will said. "According to the rules, we must start by submitting a pitch to a panel of judges. But this is good," Will hurried on, "because this is different. We have a shot here. It's a non-profit, so you know we don't have to worry about greedy and condescending investors."

I reined Will's excitement in. "We do if this doesn't work."

"It will," he said. "I can feel it. This is it. This is our time."

"Okay." My excitement returned. "I have forty-five minutes before my next meeting." I opened a new document. "Tell me what we need to do."

He talked for forty minutes, and at the end, I unconsciously popped two more Tylenol. I stretched my back and heard it pop.

Will heard it, too, and paused. "Your back is still hurting?" he asked.

"It's this damn chair," I said.

"Are you sure? Hasn't it been hurting for weeks? You should go check that out."

"I will. I need to take a proper walk, too. I've barely done that since COVID."

"Alright," he said, and then, as if remembering, he added, "how's the podcast going?"

I tried not to sigh again. I had gone from recording eight to ten episodes per week to just one now. Tru-spot had consumed my every waking moment. "It's going great. I have a fantastic guest for this episode."

"That's great, man. Alright, I'll call you back later so we can talk more about this. We need to get a jumpstart."

"Okay," I said, glancing at my to-do list and mentally struck off the discovery call for my podcast. Later with Will would be nine p.m.

"Alright, man. Say hi to Monica for me."

Monica, I thought as he hung up. I couldn't wait to tell her the good news. But I got so swept up with work that I couldn't tell her about it until the next morning.

The pain flashed through my hip, and I groaned again. This damn chair.

I met Monica on a Wednesday night at a networking event in Lima, Peru, in a Spanish restaurant called Amor Al Mar, meaning Love to the Sea. I think of the name of that restaurant fondly now because it seemed fated that we would meet there—as if destiny had orchestrated our paths and pulled us to that moment, that time, that place, with her wearing a blue blouse that made her olive skin and black hair shine, and me staring in complete awe.

When I met Monica, everything that could go wrong in my life was going wrong. I had just lost my dad and was in the middle of my second separation—a lengthy, toxic divorce that was hacking at my finances and mental health. I lost my daughters to the divorce, too. They hated me and wouldn't see or speak to me, especially my youngest. She accused me of packing my life and moving away after the divorce, and no amount of heartfelt explanation could change her mind. It hurt that she thought I would do that, and I felt guilty because sometimes, it felt like I did—even now, my heart breaks from the weight of that guilt.

Before my divorce, I'd been lulled into a false sense of security, the kind that had me believing bad things couldn't happen to good or hardworking people. But after having everything I held dear ripped out of my hands, I stumbled and struggled to find my footing. Unable to do so, I latched onto the first work opportunity that came by and escaped four-thousand miles away. Being me hurt, and I didn't want to be me anymore.

I stepped into Peru, this beautiful country filled with rich culture and historical architecture, and I expected things to turn for me, but they didn't. My credit cards skimmed my first week, and I spent the next seventeen months working on a client project that kept going sideways. I was so buried in work and trying to fix things that I didn't even get to see the rainbow mountain the country is famous for. My nights were filled with exhaustion that poured into my mornings—my days were long and filled with angst. Until they poured into each other, leaving me unable to tell the difference. I would try to call home and talk to my daughters, only to have the calls declined or receive the coldest answer. I would hang up close to tears, wondering how to explain that moving away had nothing to do with them. My separation from my ex had pulled the rug from under me. I felt like I was falling, and every day I was away from them, I was doing my best to catch myself.

I remember sitting in my room alone one day and thinking about what it would be like to stay there and never leave, to not have to do anything anymore, ever again. Afraid I would jump over a cliff if they left me by myself, my friends dragged me out of the house to a conference. I was an extrovert, and my creativity and mood always heightened after an interaction with people. But the thought of being around happy, smiling people at that moment increased my misery. Still, I went with them with the intention of leaving the minute they stopped hovering.

But I stepped in, and five minutes later, there was Monica, standing in the midst of her friends, outshining them even in the paleness of the light. And right then, I felt this relief, this soothing feeling spread through my chest, and it felt like everything would be alright again. I stared at her, wondering how to speak to her, wondering if she knew what she was doing to me by just standing there, wondering if she would speak to me if I spoke to her, looking for an opening, anything to walk up to this woman and tell her she had taken my breath away, knowing even if she thought it was a cliché, I would say it because it was true.

Then she asked her friend for a lighter, and as if inspired, I collected my friend's, walked up to her, and offered it. She gave me a smile that lit up her entire face—and that was it for me.

It had seemed unimaginable that I would meet the love of my life there, on a random Wednesday night, in the middle of the worst moment of my life, but I did, and I've been awestruck ever since.

As I dialed her phone, eager to tell her about my day, I felt that awe again, that unimaginable luck to be married to a woman who got me the way she did. She picked up on the third ring said hello, and my heart skipped in worry.

"Mi Amor," I asked. "Are you okay? Have you been… crying?"

"It's so awful here, Greg," she cried, her voice breaking. "My twin sister's mother-in-law just died last night from COVID. My sister and her husband are a wreck. She didn't even get a wake, Greg. The priest couldn't give her a wake. We had to bury her immediately because of COVID."

Monica felt things deeply. She had a way of pulling a person's pain into herself as if doing that would ease some of theirs.

"I'm so sorry, Mi Amor," I said, feeling utterly useless. My wife was hurting, and I couldn't comfort her the way I wanted. Peru didn't have the COVID vaccine yet, and I feared every day she would catch the virus. It was on the tip of my tongue to beg her to come back. To tell her to catch the next flight and come be with me. I wanted to hold her so badly it physically hurt. But I didn't ask because I knew she would never abandon her family at a time like this.

"It's okay, Greg," she replied with a sniff. "Circle of life, you know. Quick, tell me something happy. What did you do all day? How's work going? Please tell me you didn't sit on that chair all day."

I did, but I wasn't going to tell her that. "We got into Mass Challenge, Monica. Will called me this morning to tell me."

"Mass Challenge, what's that?"

I forgot Monica didn't speak Tech. Also, I hadn't told her about Mass Challenge because I didn't want to get her hopes up. Okay, my hopes are up. Telling her would have felt too real if we didn't get it, especially because we had applied at the last minute.

"Mass Challenge is a non-profit that provides support and tools to start-ups. They'll provide us with business startup tools, development training, and networking and align us with potential investor opportunities, basically giving us a launch pad to finally make Tru-Spot a success.

"That's amazing, Chiqui. So, you and Will have funding now?"

I smiled. It always amused me when she called me that. Chiqui meant "little one" in Spanish. "Well, no. There's still a lot to do before we get there."

"I don't understand."

"To be eligible for funding, we have to pitch our company to a judging panel and wait to receive feedback. If that works, we'll pitch our idea again to another panel of judges, and if they like that, we get selected for the accelerator program. If that works out, then we start our onboarding and training events. Plus, there's a huge syllabus for us to work through. And, of course, just because we've gotten in here doesn't mean we will stop looking for investors. We still have to keep doing that."

"That's a lot, Mi Amor." I knew she was thinking what I was thinking. I would have to carry the bulk of this. It sounded like she wanted to say more but resisted. "How's your back?" she asked.

I thought about how honest I should be. I didn't want her to worry. But I knew she'd tell if I wasn't being truthful. My back had been hurting since before she went to Peru, and she had begged me then to step away from my laptop and from work.

"It's getting worse, actually," I said. "I have a sharp pain shooting down my right leg, starting from my hip. I drank three cups of lemon water yesterday to help flush my system, but that did nothing. Yesterday, between the muscle cramps and pain in my back, it hurt to walk."

"Greg...?

"Yes, I know sitting as much as I have these past weeks has not helped either. And I know I've pushed my body beyond its breaking point, and I need to find balance, but I have so much to do, Mi Amor. There's no one else to do it but me."

I wanted to take a break. I'd thought about it yesterday when I took out the trash, and my back hurt so bad I wondered if I could make it back upstairs. I really wanted to take a break, but I was afraid everything would come crashing down if I did.

"So your back is really bad now? That's what you are saying, but you still won't take a break?"

"I'm thinking of seeing a spine doctor." I really was. "And maybe getting an inversion chair. It's supposed to help with back pain."

She sighed in relief. "That's good."

"The truth is—" I paused. There were a lot of conspiracy theories, and I didn't want to sound like a nut, but I couldn't deny it. "I feel like something changed since I took that second vaccine."

"What is it?" she asked, worry making her voice thick.

"I don't know. I just feel different. But I don't want you to worry about me. I'm sure I'll be fine once I get that chair and see the doctor."

"How can I not worry? You are doing too much, Mi Amor. You stay stuck in that chair all day working on the Tru-Spot app. You get so exhausted you fall asleep on the couch, and now you say there's even more work to be done."

"We are very close now, Monica. I'm not going to stop now."

"I'm not asking you to. I'm saying take a break. Do your own thing. What about the podcast? I haven't heard anything about that in ages."

My podcast, the thing I created that gave me purpose, was born in the despair of COVID. It took my clients' rigmarole and their firing me to realize I had been everything to everyone and nothing to myself. I sat at home for days with nothing to do except follow the gloom of COVID, and when I didn't do that, I moped around the house like I had lost my father all over again. Then I thought about my father and wondered what he would want me to do. He'd be disappointed that I was moping around. "Find a way to engage yourself!" he would snap. "You've got skills; use them!"

Re-energized, I thought and thought and thought until Monica said, "You've always wanted to connect with people and inspire them, so why don't you start a YouTube channel?"

I looked at her, aghast. "Everyone is doing that!"

"Well, what about a podcast?"

"Everyone and their mother is doing that!"

She sighed and gave me a kiss. "It's you. I'm sure you'll figure something out."

A podcast had felt cliché, just another self-conceited guy shoving his opinions down the throats of his listeners. I wasn't going to do that. But for some reason, the more I thought about it, the more it appealed to me. I went to sleep that night wondering about its focus, and when I woke up, I realized it didn't have to be about me. It could be about people who had made it to the edge and back, about stories that inspired and transformed.

I was astonished when I realized it. For the first time in my life, it felt like I had found something that fed my soul—that gave it purpose, meaning, and direction. Growing up in middle-class Mississippi and dealing with racism and racial segregation meant that I had to fight for everything I got, that I had to prove I was worthy and deserved to have the things I had. So, though I left that state behind and mingled with some of the most diverse and liberal people in the world, that mentality had never left me. I found myself constantly having to prove something to someone for some reason, even when there was no need to.

But with my podcast, I found that I could simply be. I didn't have to come to it listing my accomplishments or what I could and couldn't do because it became about more than me. It became about the people who showed up with their stories, not expecting anything except a listening ear. It became about the people who listened and found themselves and their experiences expressed by the featured guest. I was simply the channel through which these two groups met to connect and find their authentic self-expression.

Excited, I ran to tell Monica, and the simplicity of it amazed me. With my consultancy business and Tru-Spot, I had to ask questions that only I and the clients understood, but here, I only had to ask: how do we motivate others? And it was simple: We put ourselves in situations that provide us with uplifting enrichment. And if we are intentional and persistent and vulnerable enough to share, to let ourselves be seen, that situation goes forth to enrich the experience of others.

We spent weeks trying to learn all about podcasting, and in doing that, we realized we had so much to learn. Monica focused on learning graphics and social media, and I learned the technical and (because I am who I am) the financial aspect. Together, we made a list of friends and family that could make potential guests, and by the time we were ready to launch, Monica had come up with a name I spelled in an unusual way: Kut2ThaChase.

I recorded shows back-to-back, feeding off the energy, basking in the awe of average people doing and surviving the most exceptional things, getting filled by their ingenuity and bravery. And now, I was ignoring that for something that drained it.

"Greg?" Monica asked again.

"I had an amazing session this week with Saz Ross," I said eagerly, as if to pacify her and myself, too, because I realized how much I missed it. "You know, the artist? I still have to edit it for the podcast, but let me read something that stood out for me in our session. Hold on," I said as I switched between tabs. I browsed through several before I got to the podcast, each one before relating to Tru-Spot. When I finally got to it, I gave it a few seconds to load. "Okay, here it is…"

I was about to read it out when I paused. "You know what? I'm going to allow you to listen to it in its entirety. This is a very special one. I can feel it."

Monica laughed, and I basked in the sound. "You come alive, Mi Amor," she said. "When you talk about your podcast, you come alive."

"I guess," I said, laughing.

"Keep doing that," she said. Then she got serious, "Okay, when are you going to see the doctor?"

I pulled out my planner and scanned it.

"Okay, I have a meeting with Jackie to discuss her foundation tomorrow." Jackie was a friend who felt a lot like a sister to me. "And Will and I still have that Tru-Spot meeting with Jackson University. Then, I really need to double down and try to secure this contract with my government client. I've barely paid any attention to it this past week."

Monica said nothing to that last part.

"Then, tomorrow, Will and I are meeting with some marketing vendors to raise some capital for Tru-Spot. There's been a lot of back and forth, so this will probably take all day. I still have a ton of podcast episodes to record; those have been scheduled, so I can't cancel them. And I'm seeing that manufacturer about creating those T-shirts for Kut2ThaChase. So I'll probably go see the doctor next week."

"Next week? Didn't you say you could barely walk up the stairs yesterday?"

Did I say that? "I'll try to schedule something sooner, but with COVID, it won't be easy. Unless you have COVID, you really just have to wait for the doctor to see you."

"Okay then. But get the chair."

"I will. I'm still looking for the best price."

"Alright, love you, Mi Amor. I have to go now. They need me."

"Of course, I love you too. I will call you in the morning."

That was one of the last normal conversations I had with my wife. I remember it now because I love to go back to the mundaneness of our conversation, to the simple joy of just talking to my wife about my day, even if I was doing it with a piercing pain in my hip and COVID hovering over our heads.

I spent the next day editing my podcast of Saz Ross, marveling at her strength and the courage it took for her to find her way back after losing her mom and quitting her job the way she did. She had lost her mom to a strange cancer. Multiple myeloma, I thought curiously, the name meaningless to me. What is that?

I read our transcripts and wondered at our similarities, at how losing her mom had felt like how I had lost my dad. How quitting her job and starting all over again felt like me losing my kids, marriage, and finances in one fell swoop. I went over her words, drawing wisdom and kinship from them.

"We humans," she had said, "thrive on structure, but we are in an environment where we don't know where our next step will be. Something happens to our minds that yields itself to our most creative potential. And that's where we have to take the next step. And we don't know where that step will be. So, you know, being lost is actually one of the most beneficial parts of being creative. And when we embrace that moment of vulnerability, when we're going through tragedy, and we're having to be resilient, that's the best fuel for any sort of creative work. And it helps you not only heal faster but it also connects you to people in a way that is totally profound. So yeah, it's not enough just to make things. That's what I keep preaching. It's like, you have to also share it."

I went to sleep excited for my listeners to hear it and mentally made a list of all the things I had to do for the Mass Challenge. Will was right; this was our time, and we had to stay focused. But I woke up the next morning, and panic set in when I realized what was happening.

Struggling to dial Monica's number, I waited in terror and agony for thirty seconds until she picked up.

"Hello, Chiqui," she said, her voice tired but cheery. "How are you this morning?"

"I can't move," I said.

"What?"

"I'm in bed, Monica, and I can't move."

The 800-Pound Gorilla

"What do you mean you can't move?" Monica asked, her panic rising to match mine. "Are you…? Is this a joke, Chiqui?"

I could hear the fear and confusion in her voice, and I knew that she knew that I would never joke about something like this. She was grasping, as I was, because I too wished desperately that this was a joke, that I would go back to sleep, open my eyes, and have this be some terrible joke.

"I'm dead serious," I said, my voice breaking. "I don't know what to do. I think something is very wrong with me."

I'm not averse to displays of emotion. I just prefer they happen voluntarily or not at all. So it disgusted me to hear my voice like that, to hear it sound so helpless.

"You need to get to the hospital, Chiqui," Monica said desperately. "Can you do that?"

I thought about it for a second, "I don't think I can."

"You have to. Is there anyone you can call?"

"You know there's not, Monica."

"Okay, okay," she said and paused in thought. Then she added apprehensively, "Do what you can to get to the hospital, Chiqui. I'll get on the next flight. I'm on my way."

What was supposed to be a twelve-hour trip would take her five days to get back to me.

For me, fear is a familiar feeling, comforting even, because when you grow up with parents like mine, in an environment like ours, you learn to think of fear as the thing that made you stronger because it couldn't break you. I've been at the edge of fear many times, and I've fought through it at many turns. Stepping on and over it so much, it ceased to become an anchor and soon became a propeller. But that morning, when I awoke on the queen-sized bed, I shared with Monica, unable to move, the fear that filled my chest felt like an 800-pound gorilla, pinning me to the mattress.

This was an unfamiliar fear, the kind I hadn't mastered and had no control over, so I did the thing I hadn't done in a long time. I closed my eyes and prayed.

"Dear God," I prayed, "have mercy on me." The words felt strange as I said them, like a peek of the sun in winter, but I said them anyway, over and over, because we all get to that point in winter where we wish desperately for a peek of the sun.

Repeating the prayer like a chant in my head, I appraised my situation: our apartment was on the second floor. We had no neighbors and had formed no bonds or cultivated any physical community in the year we'd lived here because I was too busy working and Monica was too much of an introvert to socialize. Also, our closest friends and families were at least four hours away. This lack of visible connection horrified me now. I wondered how we had lived here for almost a year yet hadn't made any physical connections. My fear and panic rose even higher as I realized what this meant—I would have to get to the hospital by myself because I couldn't call an ambulance. Between funding Tru-Spot and my clients dumping me, Monica and I had been hemorrhaging our savings. It would take the ambulance at least $1,500 to get here. We didn't have that to spare.

The pain coursed through my back, and I lay there, feeling wave after wave of agony crash through me. Holding my breath through each one and praying that each wave was shorter than the last, I resisted the urge to scream.

You need to get to the hospital, I thought; you are going to die here if you don't.

The possibility of death spurred me on, and I made the decision right there to get myself to the hospital. Taking a deep breath that sent a fresh pain through my back, I scanned the room twice as if I was seeing it for the first time, hoping it held some life-saving tool that could save me. I found nothing.

Okay, I thought, breathing fast, you need to do this now. The pain had reached an unbearable point, and I could either die here or die on my way to the hospital. The only thing that was certain was I had to get moving. Turning very slowly on the bed, I crashed into the floor and screamed.

"Oh, dear God! Dear Jesus, save me."

Weeping softly and writhing in pain, a new realization dawned: I slept in shorts. How was I going to get dressed?

Slowly, I crawled to the closet and sighed with gratitude when I saw yesterday's sweatpants and T-shirt in the hamper on the floor. I pulled the half-full hamper down and pulled out my T-shirt, sweatpants, and a jacket I found at the bottom. Okay, I thought, now put them on. Turning face up, it took me five agonizing minutes to put on the shirt and the jacket. I was panting when I was done, and I wondered how I was supposed to put on the sweatpants. That would involve standing or sitting up at the most, and I knew my back couldn't take it. After contemplating for another five minutes, I resolved to wriggle them on. Each wriggle was more painful than the last. By the time I was done, I was full-on crying. I knew then that whatever was wrong, whatever was happening to me, was more serious than I'd anticipated.

I contemplated my next challenge: getting down the stairs. I knew walking was not an option. My back and hips felt broken, and walking seemed insurmountable. So, I lay there measuring the pain and wondering how to trick my body into cooperating. I moved left and right for a second, testing this way and that, and realized there was more pain on my right than there was on my left. With the benefit of this knowledge, I crawled slowly to the door, rose painfully to the doorknob, opened the door, crawled out, and let the door close behind me. I stared at the fourteen long steel steps that had seemed too little when we first moved in because I had intended to do as much walking and running on them as I could. Now, they seemed daunting, like an uphill, impossible task.

Still praying and crying, I pulled myself up and screamed as pain shot rapidly through my body. Then, struggling to breathe, I half-slid, half-fell down the stairs.

By the time I got to the garage and walked the ten agonizing steps to my car, I was ready to give up; just lie down and not get up until someone came to get me.

I had grown up in a very Christian household, with parents who weren't just devout Christians but had relatives who were men of the cloth. My father was a member of the male choir, and my mother was the typical Black Christian mom, the one who never lets you miss church on Sunday. Every Sunday at the strike of six a.m., they woke us up to prepare. Grumbling and sleepy, I would take a bath and put on my Sunday best. But it wasn't just our household. Every kid I knew in my neighborhood in Mississippi went to church and believed in God. It was an unspoken rule, one so ingrained in us it felt sacrilegious to think otherwise.

All those Sundays, sleepy and irritated as I sat with my mom in the front row, I never found God because I didn't believe He was in church. Though I was baptized, the church was the place I was forced to go to, one I stopped going to the moment I moved out of the house and started to make my way. At that point, it felt like I had better things to do.

But that day, as I drove in agony to Stone Oak Urgent Care Clinic, terrified of running into another car, wondering if I would make it to the Urgent Care Clinic alive, I thought of God and begged Him to save me. It didn't matter that I hadn't spoken to Him in years or that I had long begun to doubt the merit of His existence; I prayed. I prayed as I drove with my left foot and tried to brake and use the gas with the same foot. I prayed as I turned the corner and sighed in relief because the traffic was light. I prayed as I neared the Urgent Care Clinic because I knew it would be crowded. I prayed because I didn't want to get lost in the crowd.

When I got to the hospital, I wept as I prayed because the parking lot was full, and that meant I would have to park in the street. Doing that meant I would have to walk from the street into the hospital, a distance of about fifty steps, one I didn't think I could make. I sat in my car then and bawled my eyes out because I didn't understand what was happening. Because though this pain had been building up, today, it seemed to come out of nowhere. I thought about Monica then, about my daughters, and my mom. I was the sole breadwinner with a family depending on me at every turn. I was supposed to be at a meeting now, for God's sake! Why in the hell was this happening to me?

I sat in my car for fifteen minutes, and then I prayed again, this time reciting the Lord's Prayer from memory. The simplicity of the prayer calmed me, taking me back to nights when I said prayers with my mom before I went to sleep. Bolstered, I took a deep breath and slowly opened the car door. Then, taking an even deeper breath, I stood. Wobbling, I leaned against the car door as the morning sun hit my face and got in my eyes. I looked around for help, but there was not a single soul in sight.

Don't you dare fall, Gregory, I commanded myself as I held onto the car door. Do you have any idea what will happen if you fall? What if no one finds you? What if you are dead when they do? Stand the hell up! You can do this. You. Can. Do. This. Spurred by these thoughts, I started to make the excruciating walk to the doctor's office. Each step felt like a knife through my hip bone. Fatigued by the pain, I counted my steps to distract myself. One, two, three, four... When I got to the door, I grabbed the handle with shaking hands, said a prayer of thanks, and pulled it open.

The waiting room was a crowd of sick people, each person looking sicker than the rest. No one was observing social distancing, and I worried for a second I was going to catch COVID before I remembered that I had taken the vaccine. The CDC had announced that 38% of the U.S. population was vaccinated, and masks were no longer required for those vaccinated. But it still felt like the entire world was sick, and the sight of most of the people in the waiting room not wearing masks made me even more anxious.

Weak and terrified, I scanned the room quickly and saw the exhausted and harried nurse behind the reception. Making my way painfully to it, I reached and grabbed the edge of the desk for support.

"Mr. Proctor," the nurse asked when she saw me, "are you in pain?"

"I need to see Dr. Gogu now," I said through gritted teeth.

"Of course," she said. "Please take a seat, and I'll get right to you."

I grabbed her hand before she turned. "No, no, I need to see him now. Please."

The look on her face had me pulling my hand back, instantly remorseful. "It's my back," I added intently. "I'm in excruciating pain here. I think something's very wrong. And I don't think I can wait."

"Alright," she said sympathetically.

Coming around the desk, she took my arm, put it around her neck, and then, holding my waist, she assisted me into the examination room.

When I walked in, Dr. Gogu raised his brow. "Did your back give out?" he asked. He had been my personal physician for more than a decade, and in that time, I had only ever come in for colds and sinus infections.

It took too much effort to talk, so I lay down on the examination bed and shook my head.

"Are you in that much pain?" he asked in surprise.

I nodded.

"Okay. Please try to say something so I know what I'm working with, Greg."

"I've been sitting down," I said with enormous effort. "I haven't gone for a walk or exercised in weeks. I've done nothing to make my back give out."

"Alright, let me see." Gently raising my jacket, he pressed on the right side of my back, and I flinched like he'd stuck a nail in it.

"Can you not do that?" I asked, panting.

"Sorry," he said. "Could be a muscle pull. Can you make it to the X-ray room?"

"Doctor, do I look like I can make it five steps?"

He turned to the nurse. "Please, let's help him."

In the X-ray room, I lay on my back and thought of all the things that could be wrong. I trusted Dr. Gogu. He was an attentive and efficient physician. But this pain seemed too serious to be a muscle pull. I should know. I had several of those during my time in the Navy. But I hoped against hope that was what it was, that it was just muscle pull and all I needed was some pills or a shot or really just anything to make this damn pain stop.

Done with the X-ray, Dr. Gogu stared at the X-ray film long and hard.

"I don't really see anything," he said. "It could honestly be a muscle pull."

I let out a ragged breath. How could he not see anything? My back and hip felt like there were a hundred knives stuck in them. "Doctor, I honestly don't think this is a muscle pull. This pain I feel, I have never felt like this in my whole life."

"Okay," he said. "But we must be sure. I'll give you something to relieve the pain, and if it doesn't go away, I want you back here on Monday."

Desperate for anything that would stop the pain, I nodded enthusiastically.

He gave me an anti-inflammatory shot, and as he slid the needle into my skin, I thought, dear God, let this be it. Let this shot be all that I need. But even as I thought it, I knew there was going to be more.

Done with the shot, Dr. Gogu patted my back gently and walked out to meet with another patient. I lay there for an hour and slowly began to feel the pain subside. Relief flooded through my body, and I cried again. Two hours later, I made my way back to my car and carefully drove home. Relieved from the pain, I looked out into the streets and noticed it wasn't as bustling as it used to be. Most stores were still closed, and there were fewer people on the sidewalks. I felt a wave of sadness overtake me. COVID had taken so much.

Back home, I downed two glasses of water, grabbed a bag of mixed snacks and some bottles of water, and collapsed on the couch, my to-do list forgotten. I didn't move from the couch the entire weekend, and every time I needed to use the bathroom, I walked very slowly.

This doesn't feel like a muscle pull, I thought, as I got on the internet and scoured articles, scrolling and reading everything I could about back pain. This doesn't feel like a muscle pull, I thought again after two hours when I couldn't find anything that fit. Emotionally and physically drained, I fell into a restless sleep, the words echoing over and over in my mind: what if this isn't a muscle pull?

I tried to ignore the pain that weekend, to ignore the slow creeping sensation I felt as it crawled its way back up. But by Sunday, the pain was back with a vengeance, attacking every corner of my back, leaving me unable to breathe.

Monica still wasn't back. The COVID restrictions on travel in Peru were tight, and I dreaded having to repeat Friday again all by myself.

We had called and texted all weekend, and I told her the pain was subsiding, even as it crept steadily back up. But I called her that Sunday, unable to ignore it or play it down. "How long before you get back here?" I asked after she picked up on the first ring. "I think I'm going to take another life insurance," I said, startling even myself as I said it.

"What? Greg?!" Monica sounded completely aghast.

"I don't know what this is, but I know it can't be normal. We need to be ready for anything."

I called my doctor afterward, "I'm not coming back to your office on Monday. I need to see a spine specialist, and I need to see one now."

"The pain hasn't subsided?" he asked in surprise.

"It's worse. I didn't move from the couch all weekend."

"Okay," he said soberly, "you need to go for a test. I'll recommend someone."

That test would lead to the next test, that would lead to another test, and that would give me the most heartbreaking confirmation of my life.

Humans are naturally optimistic people, even pessimistic ones. I like to believe pessimists hide their optimism under false negativity. They have to call things as they are because perhaps if you think and say the awful thing as many times as possible, then somehow, by some power, that prevents the awful thing from happening.

But I've never been particularly optimistic, or pessimistic for that matter. I was a realist, a fervent believer in facts. I worked with numbers, charts, and data, and I had to make decisions based on that which was presented to me, that which was visible and certain, not on a future that could maybe happen.

However, as I called the spine-management doctor I'd found on the internet, I rejected my very nature. I knew something was terribly wrong; I could feel it with overwhelming instinct and certainty, the same kind that had made me successful in every project I had taken on in my firm. But I didn't want my fears to be confirmed by data, charts, and irrefutable tests. I wanted them to tell me that I was fine, that this was just a fluke.

I clung to God and optimism with every fiber of my being, crawling under them the way one crawls underneath a table in an earthquake. And it was fitting because my whole world was shaking.

The spine management doctor I found on the internet was named

Dr. McKee. After spending a few minutes telling his receptionist what transpired over the weekend and prior, she thought for a minute and asked, "Well, can you get to us this morning?"

The silence and loneliness of my apartment echoed, and I wished with all my might that Monica was here. Dr. McKee's office was two miles away, the same as my general physician. There was no way around it; I would have to make this journey myself again.

"Yes," I answered, sighing in defeat. "I can get to you this morning."

"Okay, see you soon."

I went through the agony of getting dressed again, grabbed my keys off the couch where I'd left them on Friday, and walked stiffly out of my apartment.

The drive was just the same as the last—me, letting my left leg do most of the work while managing to keep my eyes on the road through the blinding pain. It was a Monday, so anyone who had a job was at it. I had ignored all work-related messages over the weekend, too mentally and physically tortured to do more than sleep, but I still felt guilty for ignoring work and even more guilty that I had ignored Tru-Spot. We were right on the precipice of our success. This was the worst time for this to happen.

It took me almost twenty-five minutes to get to Dr. McKee's office. Anxious about the road and my back, I had driven much slower than usual. But unlike the parking lot at Stone Oak Urgent Care Clinic, this had plenty of parking spaces. Of course, there were fewer people at the specialist's office, I thought, and it hit me that needing a spine doctor on a Monday morning often happened in grave situations. I swallowed hard and pushed the thought out of my mind. Once I parked, I called Dr. McKee's receptionist to let her know I was in the parking lot. "Oh, that's great," she replied. "Our office is located on the second floor."

I paused in disbelief. The second floor? Did this woman hear the part about me being in excruciating pain?

"I'm sorry," she said, as if reading my mind. "There's no elevator either."

I hung up then, doing my best not to cry. It felt like I had cried more this weekend than I had in my entire life. What had I done in a past life to deserve this?

Mustering every bit of energy I had, I got out of my car and began the long walk to the staircase. Unlike my urgent care physician's, this walk was way more than fifty steps, and by the time I got to the staircase, my entire body was screaming in pain. It didn't seem possible that I could make it past one flight of stairs, let alone two. Dear God, I thought, at least let the steps not be that many.

However, I was met with a long line of stairs. I considered sitting down on the ground to catch my breath for a moment, but I feared if I did, I would never get up. Willing myself to breathe and keep going, I began my climb up the stairs, counting again to distract myself from the pain. But the pain was near impossible to ignore, so before I knew it, I was wobbling and stumbling and grasping anything in sight to keep myself from falling.

Climbing that staircase felt like a fight for my life. The unsteadiness of my feet and the chaos of my mind terrified me because I wondered what would happen if I missed a step and my body came crashing down. I imagined my body at the bottom of the stairs, broken and mangled, and I gripped the railing even harder. It was that terrifying thought that kept me going until I reached the top and opened the door to the doctor's office.

There was no crowd, just a receptionist behind a long white desk. I walked slowly and stiffly to her, and she raised her head from her computer as I approached. "Hello," she said.

"I'm here to see Dr. McKee. My name is Gregory Proctor. I called ahead."

"Of course," she said. "Let's get you into the examination room."

Thankful that I could lie down, I followed her as quickly as my body would allow. Inside the room, I went to the examination table and lay down. Dr. McKee, a slim, athletic, older version of my primary physician, greeted me with a smile and nod.

Pulling a model of a skeleton, he walked up to me. "Where do you hurt the most?" he asked. "Point it to me on this model."

I looked at the model for almost a minute and pointed to the upper right hip area.

"There?" he asked curiously.

"Yes," I answered with an intense look at him.

"Hmmm."

"What?" I asked with dread.

"You know there's a sciatic nerve there, and whatever is causing you this agony and discomfort is in the area of that sciatic nerve. And you are telling me that you've got shooting pain radiating down your leg?"

"Yes, and not just my leg. I've got it going on all over my chest, through my ribcage, and my side."

"Hmmm."

"What?" I asked impatiently.

"Well, sciatic pain is often a symptom of an underlying issue. It's never just a pain."

My heart sank. "What does that mean, doctor?"

"It means you need to get an MRI."

My heart sank even deeper at the look of deep concern on his face.

He set aside the model of the skeleton and picked up a strange-looking iron bar.

"What's that for?" I asked.

"Before you go for the MRI, I need to map the pain in your back so the technicians at the MRI lab know where to look for it. Lie face down, please."

I did, and he placed the iron bar on my back and began to poke and prod my back. As he did, I clenched my fist in pain. His poking was worse than my physician's, and I wanted him to stop.

"I'm sorry," he said as he finished his poking. "I just need to make sure we are in the right location. You can head to the MRI lab now, and I'll send this over to them before you get there."

"How far is the MRI lab?" I asked.

"Six miles."

"Six miles?! I'm practically immobile here, doctor, and my wife's not home yet. There's no one to drive me. You don't honestly expect me to drive six miles in this state?"

"Of course not," he replied with a smile as if he was used to patients going off on him. "I'll give you something stronger for the pain, but you need to get to the MRI lab today."

As he went out to get something stronger, I thought about how six miles used to be a light walk for me. Now, I couldn't even drive to it. Half an hour later, fortified with 800 milligrams of Ibuprofen, I made my way to my car. Monica called as I opened the door.

"How are you, Chiqui?" she asked.

"Not great," I said. "Where are you?"

"I just got to Lima. I'm about to take the COVID test. I'll need to wait five hours for the result. If all goes well, I'll take a midnight plane home. I should be with you in twenty-four hours, tops."

"Please," I said. "I need you."

"Okay," she said, and I could tell she was holding back tears.

"But I'll be fine," I added quickly. "Everything will be fine."

"I love you," she said.

"I love you too."

My nearly thirty-minute drive to the MRI facility was not as agonizing as my previous drive. I was still in pain, but the ibuprofen pill Dr. McKee had given me was like a force that was blocking it with just enough power to keep the pain from flooding through. There was still a steady trickling of pain, bypassing all the spaces that the shot couldn't hold. I could feel it just riding on the surface, waiting to come out, and I figured it would come out in an hour or so, but for now, I was grateful that I could press my right foot on the gas without my body screaming in pain.

When I got to the facility, there was ample parking space with no stairs to climb, and I sighed with deep gratitude. I never thought I'd be so grateful for the lack of stairs in my life.

Inside the facility, I introduced myself and was taken straight to the examination room, where the MRI would be performed. There was a young female technician waiting. She had a pair of glasses and an air of competence about her. She looked like the kind of person I'd hire on the spot.

"You are in a lot of pain, sir," she stated.

"I was all weekend."

"Really?" she asked. Her eyes were full of curiosity and compassion, and before I could stop myself, I began to tell her about the absolute horror of my weekend. She listened attentively as I spoke, and I could see she was taking mental notes. At some point in my narration, her eyes lit up with realization. But in a split second and with the intention not to alarm, she arranged her expression back to neutral and attentive. That single act alarmed me more than anything else I'd been through that week.

She knows, was all I could think. She knows this is really, really bad.

"You, you are way too young to be in this much pain," she said. "But I'm sure everything will be fine."

Her words didn't comfort me; rather, they added an extra layer of dread in my heart.

She handed me a robe and showed me where to get undressed.

"This won't take too much time," she said with a kind smile.

I nodded, walked into the dressing room to change, came back out, and got into the MRI table. She was right; it didn't take too much time.

When I stepped out of the MRI machine, the mood had changed. It was eerie now, and I got a horrible sense of foreboding like I did that day when I arrived at the hospital to see my dad. I realized I'd had this sense all week, and I'd simply been struggling to accept it. The technician still had a smile on her face, but it was sad, and beneath her glasses, I could see she didn't want to meet my eyes.

"You can go get dressed," she said. "We are going to get these results right to your doctor."

When I got back from the dressing room, completely dressed but feeling utterly exposed, she handed me a report and said soberly, "I hope you feel better."

I opened the report as she walked away, and it read:

Findings:

The right upper hip bone is abnormal. A tumor measuring 6.0×3.6 cm in the transaxial plane. This tumor has broken through the cortex and extends to adjacent soft tissue. At L4-L5, a 3.0-mm disc bullae is flattened. L0-S1a focal 3-0 mm disc herniation seen without nerve root impingement

Diagnosis includes plasmacytoma, lymphoma, or multiple myeloma. In addition, a metastatic lesion should be considered as infection. Recommend follow-up examination of the pelvis with and without contrast enhancement. This lesion is readily amenable to biopsy.

Note: The patient will be recalled for post-contrast study.

My hands shook, but I held tightly to the paper. Multiple myeloma? Those words meant nothing to me, and yet they terrified me because they seemed so familiar. I felt like I'd heard them before, but all I could think at that moment was, what in the hell is multiple myeloma?

I wanted to chase down the technician and have her explain to me what she meant by tumor, mass, lesions, and multiple myeloma. Was I dying? What in the hell was going on? Was this benign or not?

Twenty-four hours later, Monica arrived. Still on ibuprofen, I drove to the airport to pick her up. I sat in the car and waited for her, trying not to think much about the pain in my back. Or the words "tumor" or "mass." Or the even stranger words, "multiple myeloma." I was a fanatic at research; if there was anything that needed to be known, I was right there researching and looking for the answers. But I couldn't bring myself to type the words multiple myeloma. They scared me, and I couldn't explain why.

I sat in the car waiting for Monica, doing my best not to think about the pain or the lab report, but it was futile. They had consumed my thoughts as I'd slept the previous night and had followed me the entire drive to the airport. Thirty minutes later, Monica came into my line of vision, and I smiled. She was exhausted and slightly aggravated, and I could tell the trip had been hard on her.

She ran to the car when she recognized it, got in, took one look at me, and grabbed my hand.

"Are you okay?" she asked, and I shook my head.

Quietly, she went over to the driver seat, and I scooted painfully over to the passenger seat.

"The doctor wants me to go for another MRI," I said.

"Why?" she asked.

"They did the first one without contrast, and now they need to do another one with contrast to be certain of the result."

"And what is the result?" she asked.

I let out a deep sigh. "I don't know, Monica."

We drove home in silence.

When we got home, I was beyond fatigued. I was thankful Monica was finally here but too empty and exhausted to speak. She started to clean up the house, her go-to activity whenever she worried, while I got on my phone and started to type the words multiple myeloma but stopped myself mid-way and opted to check my emails and messages instead. But my mind was too unfocused to comprehend anything. Eventually, I put my phone down and went to sleep. This was not the reunion I thought I'd be having with my wife.

Three days later, we drove back to the facility for the contrast MRI. Within twenty-four hours, the doctor called us back. I walked into his office stiffly while Monica stayed in the reception with a magazine whose pages she kept flipping and flipping.

"Please, take a seat," he said when I walked in, and I smiled mirthlessly as if I was going to wait to be offered.

"I've gone through the results," he said. "The first and second one."

"And?" I asked, my heart pounding in my chest.

"You need to see an Oncologist right now."

The word rang in my ears.

"Mr. Proctor...?"

"Could you tell my wife to come in, please?" I said.

As if on cue, Monica walked in. She looked from me to the doctor and back to me. "Greg?" she asked fearfully.

"Please take a seat, Mrs. Proctor."

She did and took my hand, but I was too stunned to hold hers back.

"Your husband needs to see an oncologist right away," Dr. McKee said.

Monica took the deepest breath I've ever heard her take. "Cancer?" she asked in a barely audible voice.

Dr. McKee nodded. "Could very well be. I can't confirm anything yet, but you need to see an oncologist as soon as you can."

I don't remember much of the drive home, but I do remember it was deadly quiet.

You Are Superman

"It may not be cancer, you know," Monica said as I drove to morning to meet our new oncologist.

Monica relocated with me in 2016 after we got married in a simple, quiet wedding in Las Vegas, Nevada. She didn't like driving much, and the routes, lanes, and highways of San Antonio still confused her, so I offered to do the driving. It helped my mind. Navigating the roads distracted me from my insidious thoughts.

After we got home from seeing Dr. McKee on Wednesday, Monica got on her laptop and began to research oncologists in San Antonio while I lay on the couch in shock, the word cancer reverberating through my core. The pain in my back that Wednesday was particularly excruciating, but it was nothing compared to the turbulence going on in my head. Cancer? Cancer?! And what in the hell kind of cancer was multiple myeloma?

Monica called one oncologist after the other until she got to Dr. Rao's office. She was the only doctor who had agreed to see us after the first oncologist recommended by Dr. McKee wouldn't take our insurance, and the other three couldn't get us scheduled soon enough. The first doctor who rejected our insurance hadn't given us any reason. He'd simply said no. We had national insurance with one of the most reputable companies in the country and diligently submitted our records in less than twenty-fours, but he had still denied it.

Perplexed, we contacted our insurance representative, who was just as puzzled as we were. She issued us a letter to give to their billing department. "That should ensure a smooth progression going forward," she had said.

We submitted that but were still met with a dead end. Monica had been baffled by that, but I wasn't. What happened was the same thing that I did when I walked into offices filled with racist white people, and conversations paused in disbelief.

"You think so?" I asked Monica, hopefully.

"I think so."

I looked straight ahead as I drove, unable to bring myself to look at the hope in Monica's face while doing my best not to feel. I was still on the ibuprofen dosage from Dr. McKee, but it was barely holding back the pain now. It seemed the more I took, the more the pain fought back. It was a back-and-forth tug, and I could feel my body losing.

"I've had cancer before," Monica continued. "What are the odds I would marry someone who would have it too? God is not that cruel."

What were the odds, indeed? Not only had Monica had thyroid cancer, but she also had at least one family member who had died from cancer back in Peru. Maybe God was not that cruel; maybe He was. I didn't know about that; I didn't know about anything anymore. I was almost always certain, always in the know. But the pain from the last few days had upended my world, leaving a terrified and uncertain version of me.

We made good time, and before long, we were pulling into the parking lot of a moderately sized clinic. The sign above the building read Oncology San Antonio. I got out of the Subaru carefully and stared at the sign. Even with the pain coursing through my back, it still seemed so bizarre that I was here. Cancer?

As if reading my mind, Monica said again, "It may not be cancer."

I nodded with a weak smile. "God, I hope not."

Dr. Rao was small, about five feet tall, and she looked nothing like she'd sounded on the phone when I spoke to her. Her voice had been crisp, bearing the tone of a competent, straight-to-the-point, no-nonsense woman, but here she was in her lab coat, looking like the friendly mom who brought orange slices to baseball practice and took the kids out to pizza afterward. She was a bustle of energy and warmth, and her office reverberated with it.

She shook mine and Monica's hands firmly and gave us warm smiles. "Welcome," she said with refreshing genuineness, and I would remember later on that I came to trust her at that moment without even knowing it because her eyes held compassion and empathy. I had already briefed her about my pain and my time with Dr. McKee, so she went straight to the point.

"So, here's what we are going to do, Mr. Proctor. All your tests and results have been inconclusive so far, so we are going to run a bone marrow biopsy."

"A biopsy?" I asked in alarm.

Mistaking my alarm for curiosity, she explained. "Yes. We are going to stick what we call a Jamshidi needle into your hip bone to extract your bone marrow tissue and examine that under a flow cytometer machine."

I inhaled visibly, and Monica took my hand.

"Don't worry," Dr. Rao said, "you will be under local anesthesia, so you won't feel a thing. My colleague, Dr. Salazar, will handle it in her clinic. You don't have to worry about anything. She's very good."

I smiled gratefully, and she continued. "But before you go for the bone marrow biopsy, we are going to run labs and bloodwork just to make sure we are covering all our bases. We'll have the lab and blood test today, and you can go do the biopsy tomorrow."

I nodded numbly, feeling too much like a test dummy to say anything.

"Alright," Dr. Rao said. "Let's get to it."

As Monica and I stood, she said reassuringly, "You can trust me."

And strangely, I already did.

Thursday dawned bright and early, and I drove us again while Monica anxiously tapped her foot in the passenger seat. She did it so much that I had to stretch my hand painfully across the seat to steady her foot.

When we got to the hospital, Dr. Salazar was ready. She'd been briefed by Dr. Rao. We were led into the examination room, and there she was with a nurse, standing next to a bed and table with several eleven-gauge needles, small pans, cotton swabs, and scissors. The sight of them standing next to those instruments with smiles on their faces sent a panic through my core. I took Monica's hand and whispered fearfully, "I don't have a good feeling about this."

"It will be fine," she said. "We need to do this procedure to be sure. Don't worry, I'll be right outside."

Her nervous steps betrayed her reassuring words as she walked out, and doubly anxious, I turned back to Dr. Salazar. She smiled reassuringly again, and I felt a smidge at ease.

The nurse approached me with a kind smile and handed me a hospital gown. I changed behind a screen as quickly as I could, came back out, and lay down on the examination table for the biopsy.

Dr. Salazar approached me with one of the eleven-gauge Jamshidi needles, and I did my best not to pass out. It looked like an instrument of torture.

"Please lay on your left side," she instructed.

I did, and she proceeded to administer local anesthesia to my lower back.

"Once that takes effect," she explained, still administering, "I'm going to inject this needle into your hip area. You are going to feel a little bit of pressure as we pull out the tissue, but don't worry. The local anesthetic will numb most of the pain."

I mumbled something incoherent.

She finished with the anesthetic and asked, "ready?"

I didn't think anyone would ever be ready to have an eleven-gauge needle go through their bone, but I didn't have much of a choice. So I inhaled deeply and answered, "ready."

She injected the Jamshidi needle, and I stiffened in horror.

I thought the last few weeks had been agonizing, and they had, but every pain I felt before that needle went into my hip was a pinprick compared to it. This single needle pierced through and eviscerated every last tolerance of pain I had left. I gasped as she pushed it in and imagined this pain was what it felt like to have every inch of your body on fire. Doing my best not to squirm and scream, I jammed my polo shirt into my mouth, closed my eyes, and prayed for mercy.

Through the haze of it all, I felt thick liquid flowing down my back and wondered faintly if it was blood. Then I heard Dr. Salazar say, "Oh my God, this is abnormal. His bones are too dense; they feel like titanium. They are not supposed to be this hard. We may need to get him over to surgery."

The intense worry in her voice somehow intensified my pain, and I bit my polo shirt harder.

"Please call his wife back in," she added.

Monica walked in, took one look at me, and was rendered completely speechless. When she found her voice, she asked, "What's the problem?"

"Your husband's bones are too dense, Mrs. Proctor. If we cannot get the tissue sample this way, we may have to take him into surgery and put him under a deeper anesthetic to operate on him."

"Oh my God," Monica said.

"I'm going to try with the Jamshidi needle again," Dr. Salazar said, "and then we will see."

She turned to me and spoke gently, "Mr. Proctor, I'm going to give you another local anesthetic and try to extract the tissue again. Please let me know when the pain becomes too intense for you to bear."

I don't know what I said. I don't think I was capable of saying anything.

Dr. Salazar tried a second time, a third, and by the time she got to the fifth, I wished for death. Through an even deeper haze, I heard Dr.

Salazar say, "I think we have enough to test. I think we have enough."

Enough! That's all I thought, that's all I wanted to say. I've had enough, and I just want to go home. But it wasn't enough, and it was just the beginning. Because in the months to come, I would have many more instances of that horrifying procedure. And though I got used to the pain and learned to brave it, it was still one of the most excruciating physical pains I have ever been through in my life. When I got off the examination table, I was shaking, and Monica had to hold me up to keep me from falling.

As we drove home, I was fearful they would call me back for this horrific procedure again because they might not have obtained enough samples. Luckily, we received a call later that day informing us no additional biopsy was required. "Hallelujah," I said in relief. "Hallelujah."

Dr. Rao called us into her office the next day to give us the results. Her warmth and compassion were still intact, but her smile had dimmed. I remember with utmost vividness Monica and I holding hands in fear when she said the words that changed my life forever.

"Mr. Proctor," she said soberly, "you have multiple myeloma, IgA Kappa, P-17 deletion, and three mutation genes. It is Stage 3. If you have a hundred percent of bone lesions, you are considered high risk. If you are to have any chance of survival, we have to get you started on treatment immediately."

I don't know how long I sat in her office, staring at her. For a moment, it felt like everything else in the world had gone quiet, and I'd somehow stepped outside of my physical body to watch this scene unfold. There Monica was, holding my hand and trying her best not to cry, and there I was submerged in disbelief and indescribable shock.

"I have … I have cancer?" I muttered.

"Unfortunately," Dr. Rao said. "I'm so sorry, Mr. Proctor."

Those six words kept ringing in my ears as we drove home. "Mr. Proctor, you have multiple myeloma."

Dear God, I thought. I'm going to die.

"We need to call your mother," Monica said.

It was Saturday, the day after the diagnosis. I was lying on the couch, still in the same clothes as yesterday. We had driven home in heavy silence, and when we arrived, Monica had gone into our bedroom with her laptop. She stayed there for hours, and in the weighty silence of our apartment, I heard the keys of her laptop tapping furiously. I found out later she had been sending emails to her sisters about the diagnosis. She hadn't called them because she didn't trust herself not to cry on the phone. She saved that for subsequent nights when I slept, crying when she thought I couldn't hear.

My back was hurting, and my head was pounding furiously, but none of that equated to the pounding in my chest. It had been that way since I got back from the hospital since Dr. Rao told me to get my affairs in order because I could very well be dying soon. I hadn't spoken to anyone since we got back. I'd barely even spoken to Monica, and my mother was the last person I wanted to speak to right now.

What was I supposed to tell her?

"I don't think I can," I mumbled to Monica

"I know, Chiqui," she said, "but we have to…"

"Monica, I don't think I can."

My mother was a strong Black woman. A term I came to realize was given to Black women who spent most of their lives taking on the burdens of everyone around them, and no one carried burdens like my mother. Still, my mother was a strong Black woman because her strength came not just from societally imposed circumstances but from within as if she was born and made for the fights she'd won. That strength instilled confidence and fight in us in a world that seemed to constantly have it out for my siblings and me.

But though I watched my mother for years, toiling and working, turning her lemons into lemonades, and taking every shot life threw at her stoically, I finally saw a chink in her armor when my father took ill. His illness hammered at her until she broke down and fell to her knees during his funeral. Her brokenness scared me because all I had ever known and the image of her I had always carried was of a woman who couldn't be broken. She had recovered eventually, but I still caught that look in her eyes—haunting and tired. It was the look my father left her after he died. I didn't want to add to it.

How was I supposed to tell her that her first child was about to go the way her husband had? Through a slow and excruciating death, one that would steal his essence and make him a husk of his former self.

"I don't think I can call her. At least not yet, Monica. Not yet."

"Okay," she said, nodding slowly. "What about Will?"

Will. I inhaled deeply. I didn't want to call him either. I didn't want to call anyone. I wanted to go to sleep. I didn't have multiple myeloma when I was asleep. It was peaceful there.

"He's been calling," Monica said and handed me the phone. "You should talk to him."

At some point in the last week, I couldn't avoid it anymore, so I'd finally updated Will about my trips to the hospital. It had been impossible not to let him know. Tru-Spot had us talking at least five times a day. Rubbing my tired and red eyes and willing my chest to stop pounding, I took the phone slowly from Monica and dialed Will's number. He answered on the first ring.

"Hey, brother, he said. "I've been calling. What did the doctor say?"

"I've got it, Will. I've got cancer."

He went quiet for a moment and then went, "Shit, Greg. Shit! Shit! Shit! This is just terrible. This is so bad. I am so sorry, Greg. God, I am sorry. How are you …? What are your plans? Shit!"

"I don't know, man. I don't know. I mean, obviously, we are going to have to put Tru-Spot on hold. Or you could keep going. I don't know, man."

"No, of course not. I can't do this without you. You know that." He went quiet again. "You don't worry about this, brother. Go do what you need to. I'll keep you in my prayers. You are going to beat this. You have to. I'm not going to lose my brother."

I felt my throat clog with tears. "I have to go now, Will. I'll talk to you later."

"Of course. I'm so sorry, man."

I hung up the phone and gave it back to Monica. She squeezed my shoulders gently and walked away. I closed my eyes as she did and willed myself to sleep.

I wasn't sick in my dreams. It was peaceful there.

"Multiple myeloma"

I typed it into the search box, pressed Enter, and the internet flooded me with information. My eyes scanned the results, skipping through words and lines of information. I couldn't believe I was researching this right now. How was I researching this right now? I scrolled down, came back up, and clicked on the first search result. It was an extensive article about multiple myeloma being a blood cancer that forms in a type of white blood cell. The words "cancerous," "antibodies," and "bone marrow" jumped out at me, and the image of Dr. Salazar pushing the needle into my hip bone flashed through my mind. I winced.

Shaking the image from my mind, I typed another question, 'What are the first symptoms of multiple myeloma?' Like before, several results popped up, and my eyes zeroed in on a highlighted one. I opened the article, and through a haze of several complicated words, I got the gist of it: bone pain was a common symptom.

My eyes scanned quickly, and the words collapsed, and vertebrae jumped out at me. Collapsed vertebrae? Collapse? I ran my hand roughly across my face and did my best not to panic. How long had this been going on in my body? How long, for God's sake? I exercised constantly, I barely drank alcohol, and I ate right. Monica teased me about it, but I didn't care. I was in such great shape that the only time I went to see my physician was for a cold, and that was when it had persisted longer than necessary. How could this happen? Wasn't my body supposed to show me? Tell me. Give me an inkling that my damn vertebrae were about to collapse on me? I took a long drink of water from the bottle next to me and wiped my mouth. A few feet from me, Monica was on her laptop, tapping. I wondered if she was researching like I was. I wondered what she was finding.

I typed another FAQ. "What is the cause of multiple myeloma?" A series of articles popped up. I tapped on the first one, scanned quickly, exited in frustration, opened the next one, scanned quickly, exited in even more frustration, got to the third article, and realized in even deeper frustration that they were all saying the same thing: they had no idea what caused it. They knew it had to do with your DNA, but they didn't know how. All the articles made mention of mutations and suppressor genes. I tried to make sense of it, but the words floated around in my head.

I shook my head in confusion, closed my eyes, and snapped them open after a few minutes. Was this hereditary? Did my father have it, and we somehow never knew? Did he give this to me? And what about my daughters? Could they have it, too? I quickly typed, "Is multiple myeloma hereditary." Several articles popped up, and without opening any, I scrolled up and down. A myriad of complicated words swam before my eyes until one answer settled in my mind: multiple myeloma was more acquired than inherited.

Taking another drink of water, I sighed. I knew it wouldn't be hereditary. My father died from a combination of high blood pressure, high cholesterol, several heart issues, and an unhealthy diet. He had defiantly neglected his health, and I had sworn never to do that to myself.

I typed another FAQ. "Who gets multiple myeloma?" Several articles with similar highlighted words popped up to reveal that multiple myeloma mostly occurred in people over 60. I was 50.

Hands shaking, I typed another FAQ. "Is multiple myeloma curable?" I tried to remember what Dr. Rao had said about it, but I couldn't remember anything after the diagnosis. Several articles popped up with highlighted words all joining together to say the same thing: "there is no cure for multiple myeloma." My fingers trembled as I slammed my laptop shut. There was no cure? So, I could…? I could be dead in what? A year? Two? Three? The doctor said my case was critical. I could die well before three years. Or now? Could I die at 50? My father had at least lived past 60! Rage and panic flooded through my body. My daughters weren't even out of college yet. Neither of them was married; I hadn't walked them down the aisle. They were barely even speaking to me. Hadn't spoken to me in years. And I could be dying? Was I going to die?

My mind spinning, I reached for the water bottle, but my shaky hands knocked it over. The water spilled on the table and started a slow spread to the edge. How could I be dying? I wasn't done. I wasn't done living!

Monica's worried voice cut through my thoughts. "Greg?" she asked. "Are you okay? Your hands are shaking."

Was I okay? Was she serious? I have cancer. I could die! "I could die, Monica."

"Greg," she said, approaching me gently, "please take a deep breath."

"I could die, and I'm not done, Monica. I'm not done. All my life, I've done everything for everyone else but myself."

"It's alright, Greg."

"I didn't do the things I should have done for myself. And now I could die without doing them." I was crying now, my tears so thick and abundant they half-blinded me.

"You won't die, Greg. Please take a deep breath."

"I can't. My chest hurts too much. Everything hurts. I'm so close now. I finally found the thing that makes me fulfilled, and I could be dying. I don't want to die, Monica. I don't want to die."

She hugged me tightly, and I saw that she was trying to make me better, to take my pain and make it her own. But everything hurt too much, and my pain felt infinite.

I hugged her back, closing my eyes tightly as the pain from my back ricocheted through my body. "I don't want to die, Monica. I don't want to die."

Later that night, I called Jackie. I met Jackie on LinkedIn right when she began her medical leave after she suffered a car accident. Her bio stunned me when I read it. She was a nurse practitioner, philanthropist, CEO, Keynote Speaker, Motivational Speaker, and an Alzheimer's and Veterans advocate. She had worked in an Alzheimer's foundation for six years before establishing her foundation to help Veterans and individuals battling Alzheimer's or cancer. The foundation supported special needs children, minorities, and underserved communities. The final line on her LinkedIn page read, "No veteran who fought for our country should be homeless and without resources." I clicked the connect button because of that. I was a veteran who had gotten so frustrated with the red tape and bureaucracy of the government that I eventually gave up on them. It felt good to have someone in my network who advocated for Veterans who couldn't move on as quickly as I did.

Jackie was also driven and passionate about her work, her faith, and people, and we connected personally on the basis of that. My faith was nothing like hers then, nothing even remotely close, even now. But I immediately felt a kinship with her because, in her, I saw something of myself: a driven, relentless achiever who didn't take no for an answer. Her bio told of her achievements, but behind all of that, I saw a woman with an incredible and inspiring story. She reminded me of my mother in some ways, which made sense because the moment they eventually met, they were drawn together like opposing magnetic poles. The closer our friendship grew, the more we bonded, and before long, she became like a sister to me. When we started to make a featured guest list for our podcast, her presence on it was a no-brainer. I wanted people to experience the power of Jackie, and her session is still one of my favorites.

When the pain in my back first started, I told her about it over Zoom while we discussed preliminary support for her foundation's database. I had told her about it offhandedly, passing off the pain as a minor inconvenience from sitting and working way too much. But her nurse instincts had kicked in, and she asked pointed questions that had somewhat alarmed me at the time.

"Where does it hurt? Where exactly does it hurt? How much? How frequently?" Then she went, "Hmmmm."

"What?" I'd asked.

"You should get that checked out," she said.

When Dr. Rao first whispered the word "cancer," I immediately texted Jackie, and she replied with words of reassurance. Now, with the official diagnosis, I didn't need Monica to make me call her. I felt myself wanting to. She was one person whom I felt would understand. Still, she was on medical leave from her accident, and I didn't want to burden her with my news. But I needed the brand of positivity that only she could bring.

"It's official," I said when she picked up. "I have cancer, Jackie," I said it again because I still couldn't believe it. "I have cancer."

Just like Will, she went silent at the other end of the line. That's the thing about tragic news, I've come to understand; it leaves you completely speechless; there are no words because every word of consolation sounds flimsy and cliché. I felt like that after my father died. The "I'm sorry" from the consolers sounded hollow and inappropriate.

"Let me know what you need, Greg," Jackie said finally, and I could tell that she had thought over her response carefully. "Anything I can help you with, let me know."

"I don't know, Jackie," I said, struggling not to cry. "I can't believe this is happening. My head is so full right now. I feel like I just got shot out of a cannon, and I'm hanging mid-air, waiting to crash. I could die, Jackie. The prognosis was not very good."

"You are not going to die, Greg," she said fiercely. "Listen to me. You are not going to die. You hold onto your faith."

My faith? I hadn't used that in years.

"I know this sounds hollow right now, but everything is going to be alright. Everything is going to be okay. You just need to take a deep breath, step back, and think of a game plan."

"I don't know if I can do that."

"Yes, you can. It's you, Greg. You are Superman."

I chuckled for the first time that weekend. "I don't feel like superman, Jackie."

"I know, but listen," she said fiercely, "you've done this every day with your job. You just need to look at this the way you do everything else. Put together a roadmap and go from there. And I'll be here to help in any way I can. I'll reach out to my network, I'll take you to church, and I'll pray for you. I'll drive you to appointments if you need me to. Whatever you need, let me know."

"Thank you."

"Of course, Greg. Of course."

After we hung up, I sat for a while thinking until I realized what had worried me about Jackie's call. Her network. I would have to let my own network know I had cancer, too. I wasn't ready to do that either.

My mom was at church when I called her, as I expected she would be. I hated that I had to call her, that I was about to upend her world like this. But Monica was right; she needed to know. I could die, and the alternative to telling her now was her finding out at my funeral. So, the Sunday before the Monday I was to start chemo, I gathered courage and called.

"Hey, mom, good afternoon," I greeted.

"Hey Greg," she answered, and I could hear the smile in her voice. "How are you? How's Monica?"

"She's here, mom. You are on speaker."

"Okay. Is everything alright, son?"

I looked at Monica, and she held my hand supportively. "I have cancer, mom."

"You have… you have cancer?" she asked, confused like she'd misheard me.

"Yes, mom. I have cancer." And there was that awful silence again. A full minute went by, and I thought she'd hung up. "Mom… mom, are you there?"

"What kind of cancer?" she asked slowly.

"Multiple myeloma."

"What is that? Is that like a new cancer or something?"

"It's not … It's not new. It's just very rare. I'm sorry, mom." I said, crying. "I'm sorry to have to drop this on you. I know you went through so much with dad and ..."

"Listen to me, son," she said, and her voice broke a little. "It's not your fault. Your father, bless his heart, lived on his own terms. Much like you, except riskier. The doctors warned him about his high blood pressure and cholesterol, but he still ate and drank whatever he wanted. I know you are afraid you are going to die like he did, but you are not him. Okay?"

"Okay, mom."

"I am here for you. I and your siblings are here for you. I want you to pray about it, Greg. I know you haven't done that in years, but I'll need you to pray about it and keep your faith because this is going to try you like nothing ever has."

"Okay, mom."

"This is not the end for you; it's just the beginning. And you are a fighter. You are someone who will never give up, so don't you dare give up."

"I won't, mom."

"You hear me? You set everything else aside, and you focus on this, okay? I'm coming. I want to be there for you and Monica. Your siblings and I will make plans, and we will come to be with you. We are here for you, son, and we love you."

I was crying by the time I hung up. My whole body shook with unbridled anguish. Monica hugged me and tried to settle my body as it shook.

"It's going to be okay, Chiqui," she said. "It's going to be okay."

It didn't feel like it was going to be okay. How was I starting chemo on Monday? How in the hell was this happening to me? Why did it have to be me?

In the beginning—submerged in rage, pain, and self-pity—I could only ask these questions. I thought—there are thousands of people in the world, some probably more deserving of this pain than I am. Why did it have to be me? What random, unfair system had made whatever this was to choose me? But the deeper I got into it, the more I hurt, the less it became about me.

I came to realize I'd been chosen to suffer this, just not in the way I thought.

The Morgue

When I opened my eyes that Monday morning, it took several minutes for my new reality to hit me. Maybe it was because even after the calls to my friends and family, I was still head-deep in denial, or maybe it was because it was such a beautiful day. The breeze and sunlight danced through the white blinds in our bedroom as if to say, "Get up! It's a brand-new day; get to living!"

And I did! I did want to get to living. For some reason, that first day of chemo called to me in a way prior days hadn't. Then my eyes left the blinds and the sunlight and caught the state of my bedside table. On it were the drugs, the test result, the sticky note that said, "Call Dr. Rao before leaving," and just like that, I felt a wave of darkness and renewed realization hit me—I had cancer.

Before cancer, before COVID disrupted the natural routine of the world, my day began with a freshly made smoothie while I ran through my schedule. Then, a thirty-minute workout that featured long business calls. And then a quick shower and some light breakfast before starting my workday.

When COVID came, and I began my search for something new, my days first morphed into back-and-forth calls with Will about TruSpot, where we discussed proposals and strategized the best way to seek investors. Eventually, I added Kut2thaChase, and my days became so packed that leisure became a distant, unattainable thought.

My father had lived exactly like this, except he had treated his health as an afterthought. So, after witnessing the men in my family consistently die just shy of sixty-five years of age, I made my health and fitness a priority. It felt strange now to wake up and have Monica help me out of bed, help me get dressed, and support me as we walked down the stairs and climbed into the car. It felt like I was not myself like the real me had stepped out of my body the day we got the diagnosis and never stepped back in.

In silence, Monica and I drove to the treatment clinic. After the call with my mother, I hadn't spoken much. I felt like I had exhausted all of my words and all of my energy to form coherent, comprehensive words. Now I observed in silence, watching this thing happen to me, wondering how and why it was happening to me, contemplating how long it would last, wondering if I was going to make it out alive.

This time, Monica drove, and she did it at a slow, steady pace, observing even the tiniest traffic laws. Normally, I would have teased her for it, but today, her slow-paced driving delayed chemo and my new reality just a little while longer, and I held onto that illusion for as long as I could.

We pulled into the car park, and Monica paused for a moment. She looked over at me, took a deep breath, and asked gently, "Are you ready, Mi Amor?"

"Am I ready? Of course, I am not ready. What kind of question is that? Am I supposed to be ready for the worst thing that is happening to me?

"You don't have to say it like that, Mi Amor. I was just asking. Just checking in…"

I looked at her in confusion. Had I said that out loud?

"Sorry," I mumbled.

"It's okay," she said. "I understand."

I didn't say anything else as she helped me out of the car into the treatment clinic and through the short walk to the treatment room. Dr. Rao was waiting with one of her nurse practitioners, her warm smile in place, and for some reason, that irked me. What was she smiling about?

Monica smiled back at them and shook Dr. Rao's hand. "How are you feeling today, Mr. Proctor?" Dr. Rao asked me.

I mutely took a seat.

She sat next to me and said calmly, "Before we begin, I would like to explain the drugs to you and how they work. I like for my patients to be fully aware of what's going into their bodies and how it's working. Should I begin?"

I nodded numbly, and she began.

"Usually, with multiple myeloma patients, our standard of care is a two-drug combination called Velcade and Dexamethasone. However, there's a new drug on the market with exceptional results. I haven't used it on any of my patients before, so you would be the first. But it's been through several clinical trials, it's FDA-approved, and all my colleagues in the medical community agree that this standard of care is what helps multiple myeloma patients reach remission quicker. So, rather than put you through a two-drug combination, I'll be putting you on three. The additional drug is called Darzalex. Do you understand me?"

Not fully hearing or comprehending what she said, I nodded again.

"Mr. Proctor, I assure you I wouldn't be using this drug if I didn't think it would work."

I said nothing to that, either.

"Mr. Proctor," Dr. Rao said softly, "I know you are scared. I know this is not what you thought your Monday would look like. But I need you to trust me. I promise if you stick with me, I'll have you in remission in three to four months."

I nodded distractedly, and she went on, this time speaking to Monica when she saw I wasn't paying her any attention.

"This drug regimen comes with a myriad of side effects. So, besides the drugs we will be giving Mr. Proctor here, we will give you other drugs to take with you so—in the event of these side effects— you can give them to him."

"What kind of side effects?" Monica asked.

"Well, you can expect low blood count, nausea, constipation, tingling in the hands and feet, numbness in both hands and feet, fatigue, diarrhea, and possible anemia. He may also find blood in his stool occasionally."

Monica had gone slightly pale. "That much?" she asked.

Dr. Rao nodded compassionately. "They should subside once his body gets accustomed to the drugs. Please don't be alarmed," she added as Monica massaged her temple. "This is all part of the process."

"Okay," Monica said, nodding. "Okay."

"One more thing," she added, and I looked at her this time. What more could there be?

"I was going to tell you at your original diagnosis, but you both looked so distressed I decided to pace it."

"What is it?" Monica asked

"After the chemo, after Mr. Proctor goes into remission, he will be needing a stem-cell transplant."

"What?" Monica and I said instantly.

"This is standard care for multiple myeloma. It's the best way to ensure the cancer doesn't come back."

I stared silently at Dr. Rao. A transplant? Transplant?? Didn't that involve a donor, matching relatives, and being put on a waitlist... I wanted to go home. This was too much.

"You will not be needing a donor," Dr. Rao said, breaking into my thoughts. "This is not that kind of transplant."

We remained speechless.

"Take a deep breath," she said. "Everything will be fine. Don't worry about the transplant right now. Let's get you through chemo first. Okay?" she finished compassionately.

"Okay," Monica said.

"Alright," she said, standing up. "Let's get you to the treatment room."

Monica helped me up, and we made our way slowly to the room. When we got there, Monica stood back and stared as I crossed over the threshold; family members weren't allowed in the treatment room. She leaned forward, gave me a soft kiss on the cheek, and walked away with another nurse. As the warmth of my wife's kiss faded, I stood for a moment and scanned the room.

There were ten patients, all of them covered in various-colored blankets as they reclined in black leather seats, with at least one IV tube connected to either arm or wrist. Most of them had their blankets over their faces, and the rest had them up to their necks. More than half of them were asleep, and the ones who weren't reclining were unmoving, with glazed looks in their eyes. I stared at this scene with trepidation, my mind trying to pull the word that was hovering, anxious to settle in my mind.

A morgue, I thought as it finally hit home. The treatment room made me think of a morgue.

The nurse led me to my chair, and my heart was beating; I took a seat hesitantly. The leather seats were comfortable and warm, and I felt my eyes sting with tears. I didn't want to be comfortable here. I didn't want to be here.

"You are going to be here for eight hours," the nurse said.

"Eight hours?" I echoed.

"Yes. It usually takes that long to get the drugs into your system. We've advised your wife to go bring you a blanket and other things you'd like to help you stay comfortable."

I looked around again, took in the stillness of the other patients under the blankets, and felt myself suppress a scream. I didn't want a blanket. I didn't want to look like these people under theirs. I felt the overwhelming urge to get off that comfortable leather chair and go home with Monica.

A few feet from me, the nurse was setting up my drip bag, humming to herself as she did—like all of this was completely normal.

I stared at the drip bags, at the pure liquid inside them. Was this what was supposed to make me better? This thing that looked like water? What if the drugs didn't work? What if they somehow made me worse? Did that happen? Could that happen? Was I really trusting this doctor I'd just met a few days ago?

"You are in great hands with Dr. Rao," a woman sitting next to me said. "Great hands."

I turned to her in surprise. I hadn't noticed her when I sat down. Had she been here the entire time? She was an older Mexican woman, probably in her eighties. She had black curly hair and was also short, about four feet, although it seemed to me like her reduced height had more to do with her increase in age. Her face was alight with positivity and energy. Her eyes were bright, and her smile was warm, and just like the nurse, she looked like being here was the most normal thing in the world.

"I'm Mrs. Hernandez," she said, stretching her hand for a handshake.

"I'm Gregory," I replied.

"What are you in for?" she asked.

"Multiple myeloma," I said, surprising myself at how easily the words came to my lips.

"Ah. That's a tough one, but you are in great hands with Dr. Rao."

"Thank you," I said, somewhat reassured.

She smiled and went back to looking at her phone.

"Okay, Mr. Proctor," the nurse said to me. She was done setting up the IV drip bags. "I'll need you to take a deep breath now. I'm going to find a vein and stick the IV needle into your arm."

I nodded and took a deep breath.

Efficiently, she took my left arm and began to look for a vein. Finding one a few seconds later, she stuck the needle in my arm, and I felt a searing hot pain. It was just a needle; it shouldn't have hurt as much as it did, but I found myself squinting and squirming and trying to block this seemingly small pain out. It took me back to Dr. Salazar digging the six-inch needle into my lower back, and I just wanted this to be over. It felt like the nurse had jabbed a small knife into my vein.

When I wouldn't stop squirming, she asked, "Are you okay, Mr. Proctor?"

"I don't think so," I said.

"Don't worry," she answered. "I'll be done soon." She finished, set the IV dripping consistently, and walked over to another patient. She wasn't gone for two minutes when I felt a sharp tingling in my tongue and a burning sensation in my nose.

"Nurse," I said, reaching for the IV pump. "I don't feel good. I think … I think … we need to stop the IV drip."

She walked back to me immediately and bent to check on me. I reached out to her as she did, but my vision blurred, and my hands felt heavy. There were two of her, and I couldn't tell which was real. My head felt wobbly, and it felt like I was about to pass out.

"Mr. Proctor," the nurse asked, "are you alright?"

Unable to speak, I shook my head and kept my eyes closed. My skin had suddenly become itchy, and my hands felt too heavy to reach for them and scratch.

"Mr. Proctor, I think you are having an allergic reaction to the drug, so I'm going to stop the IV drip and get Dr. Rao."

Her voice sounded far away, and all I could do was nod. She stopped the IV drip and walked briskly out of the treatment room. A few minutes later, I started to feel better. Next to me, Mrs. Hernandez had fallen asleep. Her soft snoring and the whirring of machines in the treatment room were the only sounds.

The nurse returned a few moments later with Dr. Rao. She started to arrange a different IV drip while Dr. Rao attended to me.

"How are you feeling?" Dr. Rao asked. "The nurse said you had an allergic reaction to the drug."

Still weary of the reaction to the drug, I nodded slowly. "Is this normal?" I asked as the nurse stuck another needle in my arm. I flinched, and she muttered sorry. "The allergic reaction," I continued, "is that normal?"

"Yes, that's perfectly normal," Dr. Rao replied. "Some patients don't get it, and others do. You are clearly one of those patients. Your new IV bag contains Benadryl. It's to counter the reaction of the chemo drug. The Benadryl is going to make you sleepy, so try to get comfortable. Once that's done, we will wait thirty minutes and reintroduce the chemo drugs into your system."

The nurse finished setting up the Benadryl and asked if I was okay and comfortable. I tried to say something, but my eyelids got heavier and heavier until I couldn't keep them open any longer.

I woke up six hours later to a nearly empty treatment room and a halfway finished chemo bag. I would need to come back earlier tomorrow morning to finish this bag before I begin a new one.

"Benadryl and only a portion of the chemo treatment took up most of your time," the nurse said. "I'm sorry, Mr. Proctor."

I thought about coming tomorrow to do this all over again and sighed. "Me too."

When I got home after that first chemo treatment, I felt like I'd been run over by an eighteen-wheeler. My joints ached, and I held back the urge to cry as Monica helped me into the living room and onto the couch. I tried to say something to her, but my thoughts were scattered, so I closed my eyes tight and forced myself to sleep.

My dreams were troubled and repetitive. Over and over, I saw a faceless nurse inserting a needle into my arm as I screamed in pain. When I woke four hours later, my skin was hot, and I was drenched with sweat. Monica appeared before I could call her and helped me to the bathroom. When I got there, I couldn't decide which I wanted to do first, shower or defecate. But my bowels won, and I pulled down my shorts as quickly as I could and sat on the toilet seat.

Done, I got up to flush the toilet and froze when I saw blood in the stool. "Monica!" I screamed, and she came running immediately.

"What?" she asked, alarmed.

"There's blood in my stool! Is there supposed to be blood in my stool? Is that normal?"

Unsure, Monica thought for a second.

"Monica!"

"Yes!" she said, snapping her fingers. "That's part of the side effects. Dr. Rao said that's normal. That's normal, Greg."

"Okay," I said, slightly out of breath. "Okay."

"Do you need help with your shower?" Monica asked. "I was making dinner, but I can pause that and come help if you want."

I was already embarrassed and disgusted with myself for overreacting with the stool, and I couldn't bear the look on Monica's face. She was looking at me like I wasn't the same person like I wasn't the same Gregory, who had worked fourteen-hour days and booked surprise romantic dinners to make up for it. Or was that my imagination? Was this the way she had always looked at me?

So, even though my legs ached and all I wanted to do was lie there on the shower floor and go to sleep, I shook my head and grabbed hold of the shower railing.

"Don't worry," I said as I helped myself into the shower. "I've got it."

"Okay," Monica said uncertainly and walked away.

I turned on the shower, sat on the floor, and sobbed quietly as my tears mixed with the water.

When I came out an hour later, Monica had set a plate of rice and chicken in the dining room for me. I sat at the table and stared at the food. The rice was white as snow; the chicken was completely bland, not a trace of spice to be seen.

"We can't have spice in it," Monica said apologetically. "You are taking a ton of drugs; we can't have anything countering that."

"Thanks," I mumbled as I picked up my spoon and sunk it into the rice. I brought a spoonful to my mouth and chewed slowly. It was tasteless.

It had been a week since I started chemo, ten days since I broke down on the phone telling my mom about the diagnosis, two weeks since the official diagnosis from Dr. Rao, and at least three weeks since this horror began, but I hadn't told my daughters yet, or their mother, my ex. I thought telling my mother would be the hardest, but the longer I prolonged telling my daughters, the more I realized I didn't know how to tell them.

The divorce had broken them, especially my youngest, so much that she had cut all ties with me, refusing to see or even speak to me. Now, I wondered what this news would do to them. Some small part of me hoped it would be the catalyst that changed their feelings toward me. Perhaps, if they saw I was dying, it would prompt them to forgive me for the thing they felt was unforgivable—breaking up our family.

But the other part of me, the one that burned with love for my daughters, wanted to withhold this news from them so it wouldn't interrupt their lives. They could go all their lives being angry with me, as long as they were happy, as long as they didn't carry the burden of my failing health with them.

But that Wednesday, after a particularly trying chemo session, I came home feeling like I was going to die and decided to call them. I didn't want to leave this earth without my daughters knowing how much I loved them. So, with the help of their mother, I scheduled a Zoom meeting on Sunday afternoon, the only day of the week I felt coherent enough to do anything. This was all I had with them now: impersonal, scheduled Zoom calls.

When their mother and I divorced, we left things at frozen civility, barely speaking to each other unless we absolutely had to. But when I gave her my cancer diagnosis, that iciness thawed. She had been taken aback and replied with the warmth and gentleness that had made me fall in love with her all those years ago. I was grateful for that, grateful that, if nothing else, my sickness had repaired the ripple between us. We were no longer together, and I didn't feel for her the things I felt for Monica, but we had birthed two stunning, brilliant women together, and for that, I would always respect her.

That evening at four p.m., after restlessly waiting a full day for the after-effects of the chemo treatment to wear off and shuddering at the bland white rice and chicken I would eat in an hour, I sat in front of my computer in the very seat I had thought was the cause of my back pain, and waited nervously for my daughters to show up. Monica brought a blanket and a bottle of water and set it next to me. I thanked her, put on my headphones, and waited for my daughters to show up. They did, right on time, their beautiful faces anxious on the Zoom screen. They both looked a lot like their mom, but when we walked down the street together, there was no mistaking who their father was. They had my resemblance and a little bit of my stubbornness, especially my youngest, Gabriela.

I cleared my throat, "Victoria, Gabriela, can you hear me?"

"Hi, dad," Victoria said. She looked sad and apprehensive. Their mom had told them about the diagnosis.

"You look awful," Gabriela said. That was Gabriela, always blunt and straight to the point.

I took a deep breath. "Yeah, the chemo is really kicking my butt."

"How's that going?" Victoria asked.

"Well, Monica and I are out of the house by eight a.m. and back by four p.m., and I get chemo every day for eight hours. But at least I get the weekends off." I chuckled mirthlessly, and neither of my daughters joined in. I cleared my throat and went on.

"I uhm, I can't keep food down anymore. I can barely walk on my own, and apparently, insomnia is an added allergic reaction to the drugs because I can't sleep without taking melatonin. It's just one day pouring into another that looks exactly the same, and I'm just … I'm tired all the time." I paused then and swallowed; I was not going to cry in front of my daughters.

"Uhm, the prognosis… the prognosis is not great, but my doctors are optimistic. So, uhm, that's uh …that's it." I took a long drink from my bottle of water and set it down.

"I'm so sorry, dad," Victoria said, crying, and I felt my eyes sting with tears. Her face looked so much like mine at that moment. "I'm so sorry about this. I'll be here for you, whatever you need. We are going to fight this, dad; you'll be fine. You have to be. Please just let me know what I can do."

"Of course, Victoria," I said, crying. "Of course."

Gabriela had kept quiet the entire time, but I looked at her now and saw she was struggling not to cry, too. Her chin was firmly set, and she kept pushing non-existent hair out of her face like she did when she was emotional. Her screen went dark for a moment, and then she came back on and cleared her throat. And I could see she had indeed been crying.

"Are you going to die?" she asked.

That was all I had thought about since the diagnosis: was I going to die? But to hear my daughter ask me so plainly and abruptly shook me. Everyone else had told me I would be fine, that I could fight this. She was the only one who had come right out to ask the question everyone else had been dreading. I thought about it for a moment,

"I hope not," I said. "I hope I don't die."

"Is this hereditary?" Victoria asked. "Could we get it?"

"I don't think so. No one in our family has ever had something like this. It's actually a very rare cancer, and people don't just get it."

We all went silent until Gabriela, crying openly now, said, "I'm sorry, dad."

And underneath the blanket, my heart warmed. This was the first time in years she had called me dad. I thought back to when she was five and would take my hand as we walked down the street in our quiet neighborhood, pointing at everything she saw.

"Look, dad!" she'd scream in delight. "Over there, dad! Look what I found, dad!" She used to be so warm and trusting, and she looked at me with awe in her eyes. God, where had the time gone?

"I'll be fine," I said fervently. But the words sounded hollow to my ears; I couldn't bring myself to believe them. All I could think at that moment was how I didn't have enough time and how this was the first time in years I was speaking to both of my daughters together.

"Let's do this again," I said earnestly. "We could have a call every Sunday where I keep you updated with everything that's happening with the chemo and my doctors. Would that … would you be okay with that?"

Victoria nodded eagerly, but Gabriela held back like she wasn't sure. I could see her struggle between resentment and duty.

"Gabriela?" I asked, my voice thick with hope.

"Okay, dad," she agreed, nodding slowly. "I'll be here."

The next Sunday, they both showed up, but after that, Gabriela stopped. Through the haze of my chemo, I called, sent emails, and left voicemails, wondering why she had gone dark, hoping her resentment hadn't won, praying she would pick up or write back or just call me to say she was here—and she loved me. Every Sunday, she didn't show, and my heart broke until, beyond hurt, I called her mom.

"She just can't deal with this right now," my ex said. "It's just too much for her. She's still angry, Greg, about the divorce, and this is just too much for her to handle."

"Okay," I said. And after she hung up, I set the phone down and sobbed.

Every day of chemo felt like some vital part of me was being stripped away, leaving a person who was slowly losing recognition of himself. Every day, I would wake up and wish I didn't have to. Every day, I would go to chemo and sit in my comfortable chair, staring into space, losing all sense of time. It didn't help that the other cancer patients were much older than me: men and women in their seventies and eighties, people I assumed had lived a full life, people I selfishly felt could die with fewer regrets than I would. They came with books and devices to read or listen to—resigned to their fates, occupying themselves, wrapped up in their own sick world until it was time to go, except for Mrs. Hernadez, who managed to bounce into the treatment room with her walker and declare to everyone that she was here for sleep medicine. Some of us chuckled politely when she said it, and afterward, I wondered how she was able to be here with such cheer, how she was able to smile while the rest of us were shrouded in despair.

As my chemotherapy continued, I soon realized that living in this bleak reality terrified me more than death. I began to fear that this was it for me, that these would be my days until death became a release. I didn't go with any books or any devices to keep me entertained those first few weeks. I didn't want to get comfortable, but the silence and long hours stretched so much that sometimes I would go home and try to sleep, but all I would hear would be the drip, drip, drip of the chemo bag.

Monica seemed stoic, driving and catering, bringing me blankets and tea, trying to check and read my vitals, and rubbing her temple in frustration when it confused her. But I would hear her at night, crying from the weight and exhaustion of having to wait hand and foot on a man who, up until a few weeks ago, had been so self-sufficient. I couldn't bring myself to comfort her on those early chemo nights. I pulled away at night and slept on my side of the bed. I was too broken to see outside of anyone but myself.

On the days when she wasn't swarmed with errands and research, my friend Jackie would drive to the house and offer to take us to my treatments. We would sit quietly in her car while she played Gospel songs that went over my head. It was like that the first time she drove me, the second, and then the third. By the fourth time, when she dropped me home and noticed the chaos of our unkempt apartment and Monica's harried look, she decided to say something. She was driving me to chemo the fifth time when she finally did.

"Greg," she started softly but firmly. "I know this is overwhelming for you and Monica, but you have got to get a grip."

I looked at her in surprise, "What?"

"The situation is taking control of you, Greg, and you need to take control of the situation."

Was she actually giving me a pep talk right now? Take control of the situation? I rolled my eyes. "I have cancer, Jackie."

"Yes, I see that. But I've known you for a year, my brother, and this isn't you."

"Of course, this isn't me, Jackie! I have cancer, for God's sake! How am I supposed to take control of the situation when I can't even walk to the bathroom myself? I can't even sit up straight, Jackie. Do you understand that? Sitting is hard for me now."

Jackie said nothing, and the few minutes of silence that followed felt like a long, heavy hour. I wanted desperately to fill it up with words, but I didn't know what to say. Finally, Jackie spoke.

"Greg, I know this is a lot to take in, and I'm so sorry this has happened to you. But you need to get a grip. You need to treat this like you have treated every business project you've ever walked into; step back and formulate a plan of action. Your wife wants to help and believe me, that woman is giving everything she can. But she is drowning because she doesn't know how to help you. You need to show her how to help you."

I tried not to cry, but the tears poured anyway. I thought Jackie would look away in embarrassment, but she took my hand instead.

"I just …" I sobbed. "I don't know what to do, Jackie. I don't know what to do."

"I'm sorry, Greg; I cannot begin to imagine how hard this must be for you. But you can beat this, Greg; I know you can. If anybody can beat this, it's you. You just have to stop acting like you've already lost. You need to find yourself again and take charge."

Take charge? That was the old Gregory. This one felt like he was waiting to die. "I don't know, Jackie,"

"I do. I know it feels like everything is coming at you like a ton of bricks, and it is. But you are just standing there; you need to move."

"I need to move?"

"You need to move. And I know your faith is not what it used to be, but let me take you and Monica to church with me."

"Listen, Jackie …"

"Just one Sunday, one. You need all the help you can get here, and there's nothing wrong with some spiritual help."

I didn't want to go. I was too weak, too submerged in self-pity to go sit in some church and beg some God in the sky to save me from cancer. If He cared as He should, I wouldn't be on my way to chemo right now. I'd be home working, and my daughter would be speaking to me. But Jackie was persistent.

So that Sunday, after coming out of my chemo haze of the week, Monica and I dressed and followed her to church. It was thirty minutes away, on the other side of town. Jackie didn't want to show it, but I caught her subtle excitement as she drove as if she was eager to get us to church.

It was cozy, this church, small and nestled at the corner of the road. You wouldn't see it unless you were looking for it. I didn't know what to expect when I walked in. I just figured Jackie would be satisfied, and I wouldn't have to come back again.

But when I walked in, I felt this warmth. I felt it circle over me and settle in my heart. It was a strange feeling, but I welcomed it, and I realized almost immediately I'd been yearning for it. We found seats somewhere in the middle, and some of the members smiled at us when they saw we were new. I did my best to smile back, but my face felt strange like I was doing something I was no longer accustomed to.

Jackie got up after the sermon and introduced us. The smiles she got showed she was a well-known and loved member.

"Hello, everyone," she said. "I'm Jackie Smith, and this is my friend, Gregory Proctor, and his wife, Monica. Gregory has just recently been diagnosed with cancer." The entire church sighed collectively, and Jackie sat down.

"Welcome, Gregory and Monica," the pastor said. He was an elderly man, slightly older than my father was when he died. His eyes were kind, and his smile was warm, and I felt myself relax even more.

"My name is Pastor Brazil. This is a healing church," he said. "We have had members who have suffered cancer and survived it through Jesus. And it may not feel like that right now, but you will get through this. God will help you. We are here for you," he said. "Whatever you need, let us know."

I felt my eyes well up.

Jackie felt like an angel at that moment, like somehow God had placed her in my life to help me rekindle my faith because, at that moment, I felt my faith slowly come alive again.

After church, we had many people come to wish us well and pray over us. They were all warm and friendly, and it felt like I was back at church, nine years old, content to wait for my mom to say hi to the other women before we settled for the church service. One woman came up to me and hugged me warmly, and when she pulled away, she had tears in her eyes.

"My daughter was sick too, just like you," she said. "She went through chemo and stem-cell transplant when she was a child. A little girl. We didn't know if she would survive, and they told us that even if she did, she would never be able to have children. She has four children today," the woman said, laughing and crying at the same time. "I'm a grandmother. If God wants you to win this, you will. So don't you worry about it, okay?"

I cried then, fully and unashamedly, while she patted my back and handed me a tissue. "It's okay," she said. "It's okay."

When we went home that day, I felt rejuvenated and restored for the first time in years. And that night, when we went to sleep, I didn't pull away from Monica. I pulled her close and said, "I want to keep going to church."

"Okay," she said with a smile. "Okay."

Overcome by a peace I couldn't explain, I slept well that night. When I woke up the next day, I knew what I had to do. Jackie was right. It was time to stop letting this thing control me. It was time to take charge. I stood a little straighter when I took my bath that morning, and when Monica placed the bland rice and chicken in front of me, I didn't cringe. But rather than her own breakfast, she set her laptop on the table, looked at the time on her wristwatch, and took a seat next to me.

"Monica …"

"You need to sell your insurance, Greg."

I looked at her in shock. "Come again?"

"You have life insurance, the one you made the girls and me beneficiaries to. You need to sell it."

What was this? Was she…? "Are you giving up on me, Monica?"

"Never," she said fiercely. "Listen, Mi Amor, I have no intention of collecting that insurance when you die because we are going to use it now to make you better."

I shook my head before she finished and set my spoon down. "I'm not selling, Monica. If anything happens to me. If I … if I don't make it, you and the girls need to have something to fall back on."

"You are going to make it, Greg. If you die, all the money in the world will not fill the void you will leave in my life."

"Listen, Monica …"

"No, you listen. You promised me children, you promised me love, you promised me a good life with you, and you are not going to die before you give it to me. I will not have that. Right now, we have no money coming in. You can't work, and I can't work because I'm taking care of you, and you know our savings can't keep us afloat. I know Dr. Rao said three months, but we have no idea how long this will take. If you sell, we can live off that money until we are both able to work again until you are better, and we can begin our lives again. Do you understand?"

When she was done, I was crying. It felt like that was all I did now: cry. But she was right. Of course, she was; she was the love of my life.

"Okay," I said. "I'll call the insurance company."

But Monica smiled a sad smile that broke my heart. I knew what she was thinking. If the insurance company agreed to buy, it meant they didn't think I'd make it. So buying would be of great benefit to them. I looked into Monica's eyes, and I thought about my daughters and my life—how unfulfilling it'd been for the longest time, all the things I'd failed to do for myself, and I vowed at that moment to make it. To live. For Monica, for my daughters, for the life I was yet to live, and for me.

Spurred by my thoughts, I took Monica's hand. "Listen, Monica," I said. "Jackie said something, and she was right. I have been letting this sickness control me. I've given up before I've even fought. But no more. I need to treat this like I would any of my projects, and I need you … I'm going to need you to be my project manager."

Monica smiled, "Way ahead of you, Mi Amor."

She opened her laptop and opened the spreadsheet. On it, she had sectioned my chemo dates, chemo drugs, allergies, reactions, appropriate meals, times they were to be taken, and times for exercise.

She had curated links to all my test results and biopsies and even more links to the research she was conducting. There was a whole section dedicated to my white blood cells. I was stunned, speechless.

"When did you … when did you do this?"

"Your first day at chemo."

I looked into her beautiful eyes, and it hit me anew how incredibly blessed I was.

She opened another tab on her laptop and went to Facebook.

"Look," she pointed. "These are all multiple myeloma groups. There are survivors here, Greg. People made it out. Some of their stories are incredible. And yours will be, too. We are going to beat this."

My breakfast, completely forgotten, I kissed her. It was a kiss filled with deep gratitude and love. When we pulled apart, and I looked at her again, my heart nearly burst with love. If I made it out, I would give her the best life I could give.

Chemo was not as tiring that day; I felt stronger, more optimistic, and very hopeful. I was going to fight. I was never going to give up.

When I came back that day, I sent an email to the insurance company to let them know my intention to sell my claim. I got an email right back saying they could have an offer for my insurance. They attached an application form. I filled it out and waited for them to get back to me. I knew if they approved now, it would be because they hoped not to pay the full claim if I died. My death would cost them more, and they wouldn't want to take that risk.

I expected that realization to alarm me, but it didn't. I was willing to lose this, but I had no intention of losing to cancer.

The Missing Component

Taking care to manage the pain in my back, I leaned over to pick up my phone as it rang. The caller was Robert Marshall, my old friend.

"Hey," he said. "I'm at your gate. I can't get in. The codes won't work."

"Stay right there," I replied. "I'm coming to you."

"Are you sure," he asked uncertainly. "What about your back?"

"Don't worry about it. I'll be there in a few minutes."

I hung up and proceeded to look for my shoes. I found them a few feet away from the front door and groaned. Ah, well, I thought. I'm still going to walk downstairs; I might as well get started. Slowly, I walked to the door and bent even slower to pick up my shoes. I walked to the nearest chair, sank slowly into it, sighed deeply, and began to put the shoes on. I looked at my watch, and five minutes had passed. It was a good thing Robert was a patient person. Monica walked out of the bathroom just as I finished putting on my shoes.

"What are you doing?" she asked in surprise.

My cancer had made me completely dependent on Monica for almost every basic human thing—showering, sitting, standing, wearing my clothes, putting on my shoes; I almost couldn't move without calling her. I was so tired of not being able to do things for myself. So today, with Robert at the front gate, I wanted to be able to put on my shoes and walk down the stairs without having my wife hold my hand. Robert had driven four hours to see me; he deserved that much.

"Robert is at the front gate," I answered.

"Oh. He's here already?" She started to throw on the first piece of clothing she could find. "I'll go get him from the gate."

"No. I'll do it."

She paused. "Are you sure? What about your back?"

"I've got this, Monica. It's just a short walk downstairs." I said it confidently like I hadn't nearly passed out from the pain that first day when I tried to get to the Stone Oak Urgent Clinic myself. Like every day since then, Monica hadn't borne more than half my weight on her shoulder as she slowly helped me downstairs.

"Fine," she said, frazzled. She had been like that a lot lately. We were a full month and a couple of weeks into chemo, and I could see the routine was getting to her now.

"I have to prepare breakfast and get us ready for chemo treatment," she said. "Go on." Then she sighed and added, "Be careful."

I wanted to say something more, but I settled for "Thanks" and began the slow walk down the stairs to the gate.

The distance from our apartment to the front gate was two minutes, four minutes tops if you dallied on the way. But it took me seven minutes to get down the stairs and another five to get to the gate. Each step was more excruciating than the last, and by the time I got to the end of the stairs, I wished I had let Monica go. Not wanting to appear fragile in front of Robert, I did my best to strengthen my back before I began my slow walk to the gate. I was panting hard by the time I got there, so much so that raising my hand to open the gate with my remote felt herculean.

Robert drove in, parked his car, got out, and walked to me quickly. "Hey, man," he greeted with a warm smile.

I smiled back and hugged him. "Good to see you, man." I stayed in the hug with Robert just a little longer than needed, drawing physical support from it. The pain was shooting down my legs, and I was afraid of falling.

"What about Monica?" Robert asked after we pulled away. "How is she?"

"She's upstairs getting ready for my chemo treatment. We need to go back. Monica won't let us leave if I don't have breakfast first."

"Of course," Robert said, and without a word, he held me, and we made our way back upstairs.

We opened the door, and I took in the state of our apartment through Robert's eyes. There were piles of blankets on the couch. I hadn't made it past the couch on my first day of chemo, so Monica had brought the blankets to make me more comfortable, and they remained there ever since. There were stacks of paper on the dining table from where I'd pored over our finances the week I got diagnosed, going back and forth with the insurance company when we got rejected by the first doctor.

The vacuum cleaner was at the center of the living room. Monica had left it there the day before after she ran to me because I felt faint. There were shoes all around the couch, the throw pillows were in disarray, and so were the books that usually lined the coffee table.

"Cleaning hasn't been a priority," I said by way of apology.

Robert shrugged it off. "Where is Monica?"

Monica came out then. "Hello, Robert," she said with a tired smile. Her long hair was in a messy bun, and she had on a mismatched sweatshirt and pants. There were dark circles under her eyes, and, as if on autopilot, she started to pick things from the floor and couch.

"Please, don't do that on my account," Robert said.

"Oh no," Monica said. "I meant to clean before we left."

"Isn't it almost time?" Robert asked.

Monica swirled this way and that, completely flustered and disorganized. She looked … lost. "Greg," she said, "you need to eat your breakfast. We are going to be late." She started to walk to the bedroom, paused, and started to walk to the kitchen instead.

"Monica," Robert asked softly, "why don't you take the day off and let me drive Greg to chemo treatment today? I'll take him anywhere else he needs to go and bring him back."

"Oh," Monica said, and the gratitude in her eyes made me look away.

"But are you sure?" she asked Robert uncertainly. "His chemo treatment takes about eight hours."

"I'm sure," Robert said. "It will give us time to talk. This is the first time we have met in two years. Honestly, we are going to need more than eight hours to catch up."

"Okay," Monica said. She hurried to the room to get my backpack ready and handed it to Robert.

"Here. It's got his blanket, some water, his lunch, some books, and other stuff." Robert slung it over his shoulder. "Thank you."

Monica motioned to me hurriedly as if afraid Robert would change his mind. "Come eat, Greg. Do you want anything, Robert?"

"Just a bottle of water will do," he said.

I watched all of this in silence, observing how exhausted Monica was. I had made her exhausted. It was my fault.

I took a seat at the dining table, and Robert sat with me while I ate my breakfast of rice and chicken.

"That looks …"

"Bland," I said. "Very bland. Want to try?" I asked mischievously.

"Nah, I'm good," he said, and we both chuckled. Twenty minutes later, we were on our way to chemo treatment.

Robert and I met nine years before on a project. I'd just joined the LNG facility as a contractor, and my first duty was to provide an in-depth analysis of the existing integrated master project schedule and give a rundown of the impending project and all we needed to accomplish in a short time frame. My speech was short and straight to the point. My patience was paper-thin back then, and I loathed having to repeat myself. After the speech, I dismissed everyone and walked briskly to my office, ready to get down to business, but a few minutes later, Robert walked in. He was six feet tall with a full head of brown hair and a mischievous twinkle in his eyes. I liked him immediately.

"Great discussion back there," he said.

"Someone's gotta do it," I said.

He laughed and stretched his hand for a handshake, "I'm Robert Marshall."

"Gregory Proctor," I said, taking it. We spent the rest of our first meeting talking shop about energy and natural gas. I discussed the pros and cons of the new project with him, laughed when he tossed out a witty comment, and nodded in agreement when he added an insightful one.

Robert and I would go on to form a strong partnership at the company, so much so that we would get paired for every big or new project that came in. We were a formidable duo, taking no prisoners and having no patience for blubbering incompetence. The closer Robert and I got, the more I realized that we became friends because we both believed that friendship was a lot like a relationship, one that survived based on what both parties could bring to the table, what they could teach each other, and how committed they were to making the other person better. And Robert, well, he did this with an enthusiasm that matched mine.

"How have you been?" he asked as he drove steadily.

I shrugged. "Good, I guess." Then I thought about it and said, "No, I've been good. I really have." I was in a better place, and with Robert around, I didn't want to show a shred of self-pity.

I called Robert when my diagnosis happened, and he called me every day after. I still remember his stunned silence on the phone. Much like everyone else, he hadn't known what to say.

"You know, I've spent these past weeks researching," he said. "Trying to wrap my mind around this, this multiple myeloma. I still can't believe it's happening to you."

I said nothing, and Robert continued.

"I tried to look at it the way we looked at our projects back at LNG. Whenever we got a project that seemed impossible, we would diagnose it, and then research, and try to understand the problem."

"And?" I asked. "What have you found?"

"Man, ever since the moment you told me, I've spent hours and hours on Google researching things I never thought I would. I've had distant family members get sick, and some even die from cancer, but this is nothing like it. I asked Google what a bone lesion is because—before you—I'd never heard of a freaking bone lesion. What was it? What did it do? Could it be fixed? Could it be repaired? How could it be repaired? What would happen to you afterward?" He sighed. "I wanted to tutor myself. I didn't want to come here and act like I knew what you were going through when I didn't even understand it."

"I know, man. It took me a while to understand it, too. If you ask me, every day I still am."

After I told him about my diagnosis, Robert and I spent days talking into the night. And I would spend those nights talking to him as I began to understand the cancer myself. He would tell me later on that he'd written down everything I said. He opened a spreadsheet and cued up words that he wanted to research. It is what I would have done had he been in my situation. We attacked things by first understanding them. He would also tell me many months later that when he first saw me walk toward him to open the front gate, his heart dropped. "You were shuffling your feet," he said, "kind of unstable. You were twitching too, and the upper part of your body looked like it was in excruciating pain. I thought you were going to fall," he said. "I honestly thought you were going to fall."

Robert was used to an image of me, one that involved me storming out of my office into his, waving my arms in exasperation, and having conniptions because things weren't going the way I wanted. Seeing me like this must have startled him. Yet, he had kept his face impassive and hugged me with a smile because he knew how much I despised being pitied. We turned a corner, and I could see the treatment clinic now. We were almost there.

Robert expertly pulled into the parking lot and drove into the nearest parking space. We sat in the car for a few minutes, and I realized how thankful I was not to have to drive today.

"You know," I said, "you are the only person who has not simply told me that everything will be fine. You are the only one who hasn't chucked positivity at my face or told me what I want to hear. I need you to know that I appreciate that. I appreciate you for still treating me like me, like Greg."

"You are too stubborn to be anything else," he said, and we both laughed.

It was also Robert who, when I had expressed my fear of dying from cancer, had told me not to think too much about the future because forward-thinking sometimes did more damage to us than the facts.

He helped me into the clinic, saying hi to the nurses and doctors as we made our way to the chemo treatment room. When we got there, he hung back and stared. I had become used to the chemo treatment room; it no longer daunted me; now, it was simply a place where we all came to try and get better. But Robert's look of dismay made me self-conscious.

"How long are you going to be here again?" he asked.

"Eight hours," I said offhandedly.

"Eight hours?"

"You can go back to the house and come pick me up at four," I offered.

He nodded and patted me on the back.

But Robert didn't go back home. He got in his car and drove around, looked up an old friend, and stopped for lunch when he got hungry. He had too much on his mind to enjoy his lunch or go back to my home. He would tell me later on that he wanted Monica to have the day to herself. "She looked like she really needed it," he said.

When he came back to pick me up, the first thing he said was, "When I walked you to that chemo treatment room, Greg, I hadn't expected them to have you all laid out like that, so impersonal, like a damn carousel."

I chuckled as I got into the car, but he continued seriously.

"The week after you told me about your diagnosis, I was able to get a hold of a doctor friend of mine. She's a Curator for Cancer treatment, and she shed some light on your situation. She said some hospitals couldn't afford enough nurses or resources to offer patients privacy or give them a much-desired personal touch. So, they just line them all up in a large room for the day, fill them up with the drugs, and send them home. And coming here and seeing you just as she'd described it made it all the more real for me. I'm sorry, Greg. I'm sorry you have to go through this."

"Thank you," I said, and we sunk into silence. Robert kept his eyes on the road with a familiar look of concentration, the same one he had when we'd try to figure out projects together. I wondered then if the concentration on his face was just from driving.

"You know," I said as he turned a corner. "The woman sitting next to me had an episode, a reaction to the drug."

"Mrs Hernadez?" Robert asked, alarmed. I'd told him about her and her sunny and positive spirit.

"No, another woman," I answered. "The doctors and nurses immediately swung into action, and I found myself praying fervently, begging God to save her life. It was scary, Rob, to see her like that. On good days, I forget that we are literally fighting for our lives here, but seeing that today reminded me. It's not fun to be reminded."

"Did she make it?" Robert asked softly.

"She did."

"And so will you."

"Absolutely."

Robert smiled and faced the road.

"You know," he said a few moments later, "I know there are many help groups for cancer, but I think what patients need, what families of the patients need, are guidance groups. Cancer, especially your type, feels so sudden, so mysterious. It's like throwing a person who can't swim into the deep end and asking them to swim. You guys don't need a group where you sit around and cry and feel sorry about your situation; you need a guidance group. A place where you can ask questions about your situation, questions that matter. Like, what do we do now? Or what do we do next? You get?"

I nodded.

"When my little girl tore her ACL, she had that. She was able to find a guidance group filled with people who told her what to do, how to do it, and when to do it. An entire support group of strangers who had experienced the same thing. It helped her heal faster and find her way back quicker. Why doesn't multiple myeloma have that?"

As we returned to silence, I thought about what Robert had said and realized that he was right. Being newly diagnosed was daunting, and not having a roadmap didn't make it any easier. Even if all the patient and family had was someone, anyone, to help break the terminologies of cancer into simpler, less frightening words, it would help immensely. I resolved to be that person.

When we got home, Monica had cleaned the entire house and had dinner waiting for us. So much for taking the day off! Still, she looked better than she had in the morning, and her smile was less tired.

"Devastating news does come easily; however, when you encounter a vibrant guy like my husband, when you're in his presence, there is something special and magical about his uncanny ability to make you feel at home. Recently, we were notified by Gregory's doctors that he has multiple osteolytic bone lesions, the largest in the right ilium, plus multiple myeloma. Like many of us, the past sixteen months have been filled with many ups and downs. However, we continue to fight for life, peace, and prosperity in everything we do. Gregory goes to battle with an understanding of his tactical logic. We ask that you continue to be a part of his vision and legacy—not only through his podcast, innovation, or project management experience—but also as individuals destined to make a difference in this world through the actions we take upon ourselves and how we treat others every day. We ask this community and this forum to share your support or prayers as we progress with Gregory's treatment."

After Monica made that announcement on my social media pages, my diagnosis became even more real. In the beginning, it had seemed easier to do this alone, to keep my diagnosis quiet and away from the public eye. In some way, being sick made me self-conscious and ashamed. And though I was angry at being dealt such an unfair hand, I also felt caught, like perhaps I'd done something to deserve this. Also, I was overwhelmed by the magnitude of everything that was coming at me all at once.

But even more overwhelming was the reception of my diagnosis. The sympathy thrown my way was staggering. Some of them felt like empty platitudes, and others felt insincere and hollow, but there were genuine ones that cut through the noise and made me feel seen and supported. I wept at some of the messages I received and realized how terrible it would have been to fight this in isolation.

The messages I received gave me a different kind of strength and renewed purpose. The more they came in and the more I thought about what Robert said, the more I realized why I had caught this cancer in the first place. And it became clear what I had to do.

But first, I came to realize that going through multiple myeloma was a lot like buying a new house. That's what I said when people asked me. It's just like buying a house! Do you know how you find a house after searching in the market for months, perhaps years? And this house, you can see it's a huge fixer-upper, but you don't care because, at this point, you are tired of searching and because the realtor led you to believe the remodeling wouldn't cost as much as you anticipated. So you buy it and try to settle in, but you can't because a few weeks later, though you've searched the house top to bottom, you cannot for the life of you figure out where that creaking sound is coming from. And while you are trying to figure that out, the kitchen catches fire, the upstairs bathroom floods, and the roof starts to leak. Next thing you know, you are camped out in a shitty motel because you have no close friends or family you can move in with, your realtor won't pick up your calls, and you are on the phone going back and forth with your insurance company. While you are in the motel, your car gets repossessed, and you lose your only client because you missed an important deadline.

For me, every waking moment felt overwhelming and staggering. On some days, it felt like someone had shoved me onto a roller-coaster and had no intention of stopping the ride, no matter how much I screamed or threw up. It also didn't help that I had no reference point. No one in my family or close circle of friends had gone through what I was going through. Multiple myeloma seemed like the strangest, most unheard-of thing to them. Lung cancer they could get, breast cancer totally, but what in the world was multiple myeloma, and how did a perfectly healthy person come to get it? Especially one with no history of it in his family? So, for the most part, it felt like I was walking through fire blindfolded.

Therefore, though the sympathetic and goodwill messages kept pouring in, it got to me when people who hadn't seen or called me in years left messages telling me they understood what I was going through and were sure I would make a full recovery. It disgusted me that more than half of these people simply called out of obligation and not from any real sense of sympathy or empathy. But it angered me even more that, just like them, I was clueless. I didn't understand what was happening to me.

The symptoms of multiple myeloma snuck up on me before I even had a chance to process it, and the side effects took over my days, weighing me down and even terrifying me. I had spent the earliest weeks of my chemo angry and resentful, but seeing Monica take charge the way she did, reading messages from people reminding me of who I was and what I'd done, hearing Jackie's words in my head and the restoration of my faith brought me vigor and clarity. I made the decision to find out every single thing I could about multiple myeloma.

I wanted to be able to tell the people who called and asked how I was exactly how I was. I wanted to nullify their toxic positivity; I found it disgusting and upsetting. I thought perhaps if they understood what I was going through, then they wouldn't say words they thought I wanted to hear. But very importantly, I wanted to learn about this disease that had taken over every waking moment of my life. I realized then that if I was going to beat it, then I had to know exactly what I was fighting.

So, each day I went for chemo, I made the decision to document the process. Rather than come in with a movie or a book like the other patients, I came in with a notepad and my iPad to take notes. I took my mind back to the first day of chemo and tried to remember exactly how I felt during the drip, how I felt when I went back home, how the side effects weighed me down—the nausea, the loss of taste, the dizziness, the blood in my stool. I documented my moods and how erratic they were. How one minute I was lethargic, and the next I was snapping at Monica for something trivial. I continuously bombarded Dr. Rao with questions and grilled her until she had to excuse herself in exasperation to attend to urgent matters. I called the nurses to take pictures of me during chemo treatment, and though the pictures were deeply unflattering, I didn't care. The starkness of it revolted me, but it also strangely pleased me. I wanted people to fully see what cancer patients went through.

I realized the more I documented the process, the more at ease I became. The more I understood the disease, the less threatening it became. At night, when I couldn't sleep, I would pray and journal. The more I wrote, the more I poured my heart into my little black notebook and the more clarity and strength I got. I stopped looking at chemo with foreboding and doom. It became a place where I went to reflect, to try and understand what was happening to me. It also became the place where I wrote the most inspiring things for myself and for others.

The more I learned about multiple myeloma, the more I realized there was not enough information about it. It was such a rare cancer that not enough attention was given to it. I wondered why. Perhaps if more people knew about it, they could stop the cancer before it happened. It seemed unrealistic, this thought of mine, but the thought of anyone else going through what I was going through left me angry and empathetic. And these feelings fueled my motivation.

For her part, Monica took to managing my disease earnestly. She monitored every symptom, making sure my vitals and labs were average. She was meticulous about sticking to the exercise routine she'd created for us, scheduling days and times for us to walk the trails close to our apartment. She'd gotten the idea from the various multiple myeloma groups she joined that encouraged exercise and even set targets to motivate us. "We need to keep you active," she said on our first day on the trails. "I don't want you spending every weekend after chemo laid out on the couch. We need to keep your strength up."

Robert had jokingly called her my project manager, which had me laughing because that's exactly what Monica and I had been going for. However, when I sobered, I realized I was so used to managing everything and being in charge that although I'd suggested it in the beginning, it had felt strange and impotent to be managed. But eventually, I was grateful for it, thankful to have a wife who didn't sleep at night until she was sure I was alright.

Once, on a sunny, airy day, as we walked the trails, I told Monica I wanted to start posting about my cancer journey. She looked at me aghast.

"You can't do that," she said. "What is happening to you is private and should be kept so. It's one thing to announce to your network; it's another to lay it all bare. They don't need to know every detail."

Monica came from a culture that kept their personal troubles secret from anyone who wasn't family. Everything was kept close to the chest and was only revealed on a need-to-know basis. She hadn't told anyone outside of her family when she'd had thyroid cancer. The only reason I knew was because eighteen years later, she still took thyroid medication. Normally, I would agree with her. I didn't believe in sharing my business, but this felt different.

I did my best to explain it to her. "I've thought about this, Monica. This is something I need to do, Mi Amor. I feel like, I feel like it's a purpose I have to fulfill."

"A purpose?" she asked skeptically. I knew she was thinking about the podcast. That had felt purposeful, too, before I'd let Tru-Spot overwhelm it.

I went silent as I tried to form the words in my head. But then I remembered what Robert said about multiple myeloma patients needing groups, support, and guidance, and it came easier than I expected.

"Yes, a purpose. I have felt lost since this cancer began, lost and afraid that I was going to die. But ever since church, ever since rekindling my faith and finding my way to God, and then Robert's visit, I have felt filled with a sense of purpose that I cannot describe. And I feel like a huge part of it is sharing my story with people. There are millions of people out there with this disease who do not understand it and feel alone and defeated. I mean, look how people reacted when we announced it to my network. More than half of them didn't even know what multiple myeloma was. More people need to know about this, and the people who already do, who are going through it just like I am, need to feel less alone. And if I can reach just one person, if I can let that one person know that I get it, if I can make them feel less alone, then I would have done something worthy, something right."

Monica looked at me deeply then, and I understood the look because, like her, I had never heard such fervent passion in my voice before.

"Okay," she said slowly as if she was turning her answer over in her mind. "If this is something you have to do."

"You should do a segment on the podcast, too," she said after some moments of silence. "I think it would be beneficial to your listeners."

So, I started to share my journey online. Every day, I posted something, perhaps a picture of an overwhelming chemo session, along with a post. Other days, I would post something I thought was inspiring. And then, on some other days, I posted about God. It always surprised me when I did that; I never believed I could be someone who posted so boldly about my faith. It was liberating; it was everything.

With Monica by my side, we ran a podcast episode, educating people on what kind of cancer it was and how it could be diagnosed. We spent an enormous amount of time researching, learning all we could about the sickness so we could share as much as we could. The more I read up on multiple myeloma, the more I realized it was quite hard to detect, and the best way to stay on top of it was to get tested as frequently as possible. So Monica and I reached out to podcasters I'd formed a relationship with, contacts from Tru-Spot and my network, to raise awareness about multiple myeloma and the need for increased routine medical checkups. Our aim was to create a safe haven for people diagnosed with the disease, to share resources and tips to prevent future cases, to provide financial aid for people struggling with the disease, and to establish a single point of facts, information, and resources so people in need could dip into our archives and come away with whatever they needed. We leveraged multiple myeloma organizations and foundations to help create a podcast series focused on highlighting information from doctors and scientists studying this cancer and closing the gap as to why multiple myeloma was twice as common and deadly in the Black community.

Through all this, I kept on posting, sharing, and learning more about the disease, and the more I did, the more people connected with it. It started small, comment here or there, and soon, people were sending emails, telling me how my posts had found them and pulled them back from the edge. It amazed me that my story could touch a person so deeply they felt pulled back from the edge; it amazes me still. Eventually, I got to the point where people asked, "What's multiple myeloma like?"

And I'd say, "It's the best thing that happened to me." And when in shock, they asked why, I answered, "It grounded me, humbled me, took me to a place where I was able to place people first in a different, more fulfilling way."

I no longer gave everything and left nothing for myself because now the only thing I had to give was my story, the vulnerability of letting others know that I hurt too, just like them. That I wasn't Superman, that I struggled, and this cancer was kicking my butt—but damn if I wasn't kicking back. And it turned out that that was enough.

We tend to create a version of ourselves that we think people around us want, but in the end, the only thing we need to give is the vulnerability and strength of being our true selves.

I had been posting for several weeks when, on one of our nightly calls, Robert asked me a question—a question that brought me to a new realization. We'd been talking for almost an hour when he suddenly asked, "Is it a crutch?"

"Is what a crutch?"

"Your new-found faith. I mean, I admire how vulnerable you are on your social media and podcast and how you talk about your faith and God with such ease. But many people, when faced with life-threatening situations, run back to God and their faith and hold on to it like a crutch, making it impossible for them to think or do anything for themselves. And I know you've never been one to rely on anyone but yourself, much less a higher power you can't even see. So, it made me wonder if these posts, this new belief, was a crutch."

I went quiet. I was hurt by what Robert had said because…was he saying I couldn't think for myself? I had become one of those docile religious people who attributed even the most logical, explainable thing to a higher, mysterious power. And it was ironic, too, that he questioned my vulnerability and faith when his words had contributed to helping me lay them bare.

But then, I saw how this new-found faith could look like a crutch to a person who had known me as long as Robert had. Robert wasn't spiritual or religious. Much like me, he had always dealt with facts and things he could see and control. So, I understood why this was confusing for him, why it felt like I was grasping at straws.

I smiled. "No, Robert. It's not a crutch. It's the missing component."

"What?"

"I found the missing component."

"What do you mean?"

I took a deep breath. "From the moment my cancer began, from the moment I got my diagnosis, I questioned everything; my foremost question was, "Why? Why me?" It made no sense to me. On the one hand, I felt targeted, like the kid in school the bullies took perverse pleasure in torturing. On another, it felt random, like I'd been singled out by a bored God who took pleasure in watching its subject suffer.

For every unhealthy choice my father and his father before him had made, I'd made the opposite. I ate right and exercised even better. I was going to live past my sixties. I told myself I was not going to go the way of my father and his fathers, all those men who had stared death in the face just shy of sixty and succumbed.

"So, when cancer came knocking and laughing in my face, reminding me there was a thing called fate and I had no control over it, I cowered and asked questions but didn't get answers. Every day after chemo, I came home and lay on the couch, trapped in this place where nothing mattered, where the only thing that rang true to me was my inevitable death. It didn't matter that the doctors seemed optimistic; it didn't matter that Monica had called her family, and they had started a prayer circle for me in Peru that ran every morning. I was angry and depressed, and every positive, generic remark made me even angrier and more depressed. Why pray? I thought. If God was going to stand by and do nothing, why pray if it appeared that your fate was already decided?

But Jackie took me to church, and the moment I stepped into that church, it felt like my heart opened; it felt like God was waiting at the door to answer my questions. I had assumed that God had stood by and let this happen to me, but God never stands by to let anything happen. And while this realization stunned me, it also upset me because if He never stood by and let anything happen, then why was this happening to me?

And that's when I got my answer. I was trapped, but not in the place I thought I was. I had assumed arrogantly that I was too good for cancer, that I was above it. That I was too smart and strong and different to go through the trials and worries normal, lesser people went through. Over two million people in the United States get sick with cancer every year, and I had assumed that I was better than all of them.

I had assumed too that I had found my purpose, first with my consultation business, then with Tru-Spot, and then with the podcast. Yes, I wanted to tell stories, and I wanted to inspire people, but my vision lacked one important component: God. The God from the faith I'd abandoned all those years before, the God whom I now called on angrily because He had let this happen to me. He was and had been the missing component.

I was just too wrapped up in the life I had created for myself, in materialism and self-centeredness, to acknowledge or see Him."

I paused. Robert had gone completely silent, but I could hear him breathing. I continued.

"That day after I came back from the church, I felt a pause and a softening in my heart. I came to a crucial realization that this cancer wasn't happening to me; it was happening to me. And so, my question changed from 'Why me?' to 'Why not me?' There was no randomness in the two million because each one has a story, and the thing that crowned their journey was how that experience changed them and affected others."

Robert remained silent, and I wondered if he was there. Then he said in complete awe, "Wow."

I smiled. "Wow, indeed."

The Myth, The Man, The Legend

I was just settling into my first two months of chemo treatment when Laura from the accounting department of Oncology San Antonio contacted me. It was a Friday. I had just returned from my chemo session, and Monica was working on her computer in the bedroom. Laura's voice was gentle, almost friendly even, yet I felt an eerie feeling as if a strong tsunami wave was about to come crashing down on me.

"Mr. Proctor," she said after mild pleasantries, "your primary healthcare insurance provider has not made a payment to any of our claims in the last month."

Too astounded to speak, I muttered, "What?"

"Yes, Mr. Proctor"

"Are you … are you sure?" I said more audibly.

"Very. I'm staring at your records now. It's not looking good. I don't want to say you are in a precarious position, but that appears to be the issue. Your bill has exceeded $250,000. We are being forced to halt your treatment due to lack of payment."

"$250..?" My mind went numb for a moment. "There has to be some mistake," I said when I recovered. "There has to be."

"There is no mistake, Mr. Proctor. Perhaps you should consult your healthcare provider."

"I will. I will. Thank you."

"Of course, Mr. Proctor. Have a great weekend."

My hands shook as I set the phone down. $250,000? $250,000? No. There had to be a mistake. There had to be. I picked up my phone and dialed the number of my healthcare provider and was immediately put on hold. I walked to our bedroom as the music played. There had to be some mistake; there had to be. Monica looked up with a smile on her face as I walked in, but her smile faltered when she saw the look on my face.

"What's wrong?" she asked in alarm. "Did something ..? Was that Dr. Rao?"

I took the phone off my ear. The hold music was grating on my nerves.

"No, it was Laura from accounting."

"And?"

"She said our insurance hasn't approved our claim in the last month. She says we owe $250,000."

"Dear God!"

I put the phone back to my ear. The music was still on.

"How did that—?" Monica started. "When did that—? Can they do that? Can they just stop paying without telling you?"

Monica wasn't conversant with Laura or the mechanics of the American healthcare system. And at that moment, I wasn't sure I understood much either.

"They've put me on hold," I said. "I'm trying to call them, but they've kept me on hold."

Moni stared at the watch I'd given her on our last anniversary. "It's past four p.m.," she said. "There's probably no one at the office."

"This can't wait till Monday," Monica said. "They are halting treatment."

"Oh God, they can't do that. Dr. Rao wouldn't let them do that, would she?"

"I don't know. It may not be up to her."

Even though Monica said there was probably no one at the office, I spent the weekend calling my healthcare provider, and they kept me on hold the entire time. By Sunday, I was frustrated and anxious, and by Monday, I had a sinking fear in my stomach. What if I went and they refused to administer chemo to me? What would I do then? But chemo went without a hitch on Monday. The nurse efficiently connected the drip to the Medi port I'd had installed a week earlier (a wonderful alternative to searching for a vein every time I needed to get hooked to the IV) and walked away to attend to other patients. Still, I sat there uneasily.

After we arrived home, I spent three hours battling side effects and trying to sleep off the chemo. Somewhat stable five hours later, I sat on the couch, shrouded in a blanket, and called the insurance company. They immediately put me on hold again. Impatiently, I waited for them to come back on; again, their hold music was really grating on my very frazzled nerves.

"What's this about you people not covering my treatment?" I asked the moment someone picked up. I wanted to sound stern, but the effects of the chemo just made me sound weak and tired.

"Mr. Proctor, my name is Jane. I'll be attending to you today. We were so sorry to hear about your diagnosis."

Right, I bet they were. "What's going on with my coverage? I have been paying my premiums steadily for the past five years, and I've barely used it."

"We are in the process of approving payment; we just need to do an internal audit of your claim."

"An internal audit?" I ran my hand roughly across my face. "And how long is that going to take?"

"We are being as fast as we can, Mr. Proctor."

"Well, you need to be faster. If these payments don't get approved, I'll have to stop chemo, and I can't afford to do that."

"Alright, Mr. Proctor, thank you, and again, so sorry about your cancer."

"Thank you," I said and hung up.

I waited the next few days to hear from them but didn't. By the weekend, my oncologist reminded me of the approval again and told me about our bill.

"This week alone has cost $22,500."

I swallowed hard. "We are in talks with our healthcare provider. They should get back to us soon."

"I hope so," she said. "We cannot afford to stop your chemo. We would lose all the progress we've already made."

By the end of that week, my insurance company still hadn't gotten back to me, and I decided I couldn't simply walk into the treatment room on Monday and expect to be treated. After chemo that day, Monica and I made our way to Laura's office. Laura was a blond, five-foot-four Latina woman sitting on a white chair and typing behind a white laptop and white desk. Her walls were white, and so were the stacks of files on the left side of her table. Behind her was a white bookshelf with several rows of colored books to compliment the white. She smiled when she saw us, and that gave me hope.

"Take a seat," she said when we entered.

Careful not to stain the sparkling white seats, Monica and I sat. Monica went straight to business. "What can we do to keep his treatment going?

Laura thought for a moment. "Well," she said finally, "if you guys could come up with $10,000 in good faith, that would buy you more time. The clinic would keep providing you with treatment until the issue with your primary health care is resolved."

Monica sighed. We didn't have a thousand dollars between us.

"Do we have to pay it at once?" I asked. "What if we paid $5,000 now and $5,000 in two weeks?" I had no idea where I was going to pull the cash from, but my mind was already turning. Maybe the insurance company would be done with their audit by then.

"That could work," Laura said. "Yeah, if you can do that, we will keep your chemo going. But you have to pay the $5,000 before chemo on Monday."

Monica and I thanked her and walked out. We rushed home as fast as we could and called the insurance company, and again, I was put on hold.

"What is going on?" I asked, beyond frustrated when they finally picked up. I had been kept on hold for nearly an hour.

"Hello, Mr. Proctor, how are you doing today?" It was Jane again.

I ignored her greeting. "Listen, my doctors are yet to get approval on my previously submitted claims; we need these payments. You said you needed to do an internal review before you could approve my payments. How long is that going to take?"

"We have actually finished with that."

I sighed a huge sigh of relief, closed my eyes, and massaged my temples slowly. I had begun to do that whenever I felt the urge to throw up. "Okay, when will payments resume?" I asked.

"It can't, not yet."

"I don't understand."

"We need you to pay a fifteen-thousand dollar deductible before we can begin covering your payments."

My eyes snapped open. There was no way my deductible was that much.

"What exactly are you saying?" I asked. "I've been paying a premium of $800 a month for years now."

"Well, our coverage only extends seventy percent. According to your agreement, you have to pick up the remaining thirty percent."

"Listen," I said, my voice taking on an imploring tone, "I cannot afford that deductible right now. If you don't pay for my treatment, I will have to stop chemo, and if I stop chemo, I'll die. Do you understand me? I'm not in any position to pay that money right now because I have no income coming in. I haven't since COVID, and the chemo makes it impossible for me to work. Is there nothing you people can do?"

"Perhaps you'd like to talk to your insurance manager?" Jane said.

I sighed. "Okay."

"Okay, please hold while I put you through." I held for about an hour before I realized I would not be talking to anyone else from the insurance company that day.

"What are we going to do, Greg?" Monica asked me that night as we tried to go to sleep. I was too distressed to answer her. The sale of my life insurance was still going through, and they hadn't gotten back to me yet. I refreshed my email a dozen times in the past week to check. A year ago, fifteen thousand would have been nothing; now, there was really no way I could afford to pay that.

In 2019, tired of living in an apartment, Monica and I decided to buy a house. We had about $150,000 in savings and felt confident we would get something great. We found a realtor and applied for a loan, dropped $5,000 for them to take the house off the market, and got approved. The week we were about to move in, we were told we weren't approved. The bank didn't want to give the loan until they ensured my company, SchXer, which I started the year before and had been in operation for two years. It hadn't, so we skipped the bank and found another lender. I felt the bank was being unrealistic. They were basing the loan on my company, SchXer, but I wasn't buying the house under my company. I was buying it under Gregory Proctor.

However, this lender gave us the run-around. They would tell us we had been approved and tell the sellers a different thing. On and on, it went until Monica, who was trying to get a job, started to think I was giving her the runaround. I explained to her that I was just as frustrated as she was.

Eventually, the lenders insisted we had a line of credit in my business and had to pay that off before they could approve the loan.

They insisted we had to pay that, plus my existing tax bill of $90,000 for the current year. We paid but had to utilize our savings to do it. At that point, I was beyond frustrated.

Even with that paid, the back and forth with the lenders went on for weeks. The sellers of the house became frustrated and distrustful because they thought we were giving them the runaround, too, until, in frustration, they dropped our offer. But at that point, they had taken the house off the market for months, and we couldn't recover our down payment, so our $5,000 went poof. That and the tax bill of $90,000, which the lenders insisted we pay, wrecked our savings. Between that, funding Tru-Spot, and the eventual barrenness wrought by COVID, we barely had any savings left and no money coming in. Eventually, we ended up in a small apartment, utterly dissatisfied and furious at the money we had lost.

That night, I tossed and turned and wondered whom I could ask for a loan, but the very thought nauseated me. I had never had to ask anyone for help before. I wouldn't even know where to start. Tired and afraid, I fell into a restless sleep. The next morning, Monica woke me up.

"I'm going to contact my family and ask them to help."

"Monica …"

"They will help, Gregory. I should have asked them all this time."

"I don't doubt they will help." Monica's family was some of the most generous people I'd ever met. "But $15,000 is a lot to ask anyone right now. People are struggling."

"Oh, no," Monica said, aghast. "We are not going to ask them for the deductible."

"We aren't?"

"No, and we are not going to ask them for Laura's $10,000 either."

"No?"

"Gregory, we are completely out of money here. We won't be able to afford gas or groceries soon. That's what I'm going to ask for. You need to put Laura's money on your credit card."

"Our personal credit cards?"

"No. We are completely maxed out. Your business one."

I looked at her in astonishment; how hadn't I thought of that? The insurance company wouldn't take credit cards, but Laura would.

"It's okay," Monica said when she saw the astonished look on my face. "You have a lot on your mind. I'll send a message to my family now." She did, and they came through for us, enough that by economizing, we had groceries and gas for two months.

The next day, Monica and I went to Laura and put $5,000 on my business credit card. "We will pay the rest in two weeks," I said.

"No worries," Laura replied compassionately. "I hope everything works out with your insurance."

"Me too," I said. We had three weeks to a month to restart normal payments again. Where were we supposed to get $15,000?

Every day that week after chemo, I tried to get through to the insurance people, but they were very clear on their demand: no deductible, no coverage. All this while, I was combating the side effects of my chemo. I slammed my phone down in frustration more than a few times. Were these people going to let me die over a deductible even though I had been consistent with my premiums for years? But more than that, I was furious because almost a year back, I would have paid this deductible in my sleep. When did I become someone who couldn't afford a $15,000 deductible? When did I become someone who had no money?

By the end of the month, Laura was getting anxious, and I was drowning in bills and pressure. Until Jackie reached out with a solution I hadn't even considered: the Veterans Hospital.

Joining the Navy after high school had been a no-brainer for me. Growing up in Brandon, Mississippi, the one thing that stood out to me was the complacency. I knew there was a whole life outside our small, often narrow-minded town, but everyone else acted like living, growing, and dying there was the best there was. As if the concept of more was only reserved for the people we saw on TV and in newspapers. As if those people were so far removed, they were mini-Gods. I would watch older friends and acquaintances go off to college only to come back and work in the Burger King down the block. The more I saw this, the more I swore it would never be me. So, on the day I got my high school diploma, I set it before my parents and told them I would be joining the Navy. My mother had looked at me aghast, but my father had nodded in approval, one of the few times he ever did.

"Go on, son," he said proudly. "Go make something of yourself."

Off I went, with only a small backpack and my mother's kiss on my forehead. I served and afterward took advantage of the GI bill to pay my way through college. After that, I took no other benefit from the government. I was eager to start up my life, eager to get acquainted with the real world outside Brandon and the U.S. Navy. And I did.

The farther I went and the more money I made, the smaller these places became. I never applied for the Veterans benefits, never even considered it. I was making so much money that I felt whatever they gave me would pale in comparison. So, it felt surreal to be driving to the Veterans Hospital after chemo, hoping to get assistance from them to pay for my chemo. It embarrassed me to need this place after thinking I never would.

Jackie had emailed and called her contact, Tony, ahead, so as we pulled into the parking lot, we expected him to be waiting for us there. He wasn't. Thankfully, my face cap shielded my face from the sun as I sat on the steps, waiting, with my hands supporting my head as Jackie called him to let him know we had arrived. I was so dizzy I feared I would fall asleep right there on the steps. A few minutes later, Tony came bounding out of the building. He looked to be in his mid-fifties, of Mexican heritage, and had curly salt-and-pepper hair. He had a big smile on his face and a deep baritone voice.

He stretched out his hand for a handshake, but too weak to take it, I nodded a greeting. Jackie and Monica shook his hand gratefully. He and Jackie exchanged even more pleasantries, and I could see that they shared a mutual respect for each other.

"Nice T-shirt," he said to me.

"Thanks," I said weakly. My black shirt had the words, The Myth, The Man, The Legend written on it. I hadn't even been aware when I picked it out that morning.

"Is he coherent enough?" Tony asked Jackie. "Because he will need to fill out some forms for registration, and I don't know... he looks..."

"Can you fill out some forms?" Jackie asked.

If filling out forms was all I needed to do to get the money for my chemo, I would fill out all the forms in the world. Nodding slowly, I stood so they knew I was serious.

"Alright," Tony said with a smile. He turned, and we followed him into the lobby of the VA hospital. It was a large white room with plenty of tables and chairs for those waiting to see a registration coordinator. I had expected as much, but its appearance still appeared quite plain to me. It was nothing like the soft hues of Dr. Rao's clinic. There were two stands on the sides of the room with essential pamphlets, brochures, and personnel resources to help guide you. I pulled one and scanned it.

Tony introduced us to some people in the lobby, letting them know I was a veteran who had just been diagnosed with stage-three multiple myeloma. After that, he took me to the intake coordinator—a middle-aged woman whose name badge read Delan.

"He needs to get back into the VA system," Tony said to her after a friendly greeting. It was clear he was well-known and liked here.

Delan smiled, motioned me towards a seat, and gave me a number.

"I've got an appointment with my oncologist in half an hour, so I can't stay," Tony said after we had gotten situated. He was a cancer survivor, and the VA was covering his payments. "Let me know how it goes," he said to Jackie.

"Sure." She shook his hand again, and he left. Alone, we waited for forty-five minutes before my number was called.

"Please follow me," Delan said. Monica and Jackie waited in the lobby as I followed her into an office down the hall. When we got there, she offered me a seat and gave me some forms to fill out. I filled them out as quickly as I could and handed them back to her.

"Can I see your identification?" she asked.

I opened the file I came with and presented a copy of my DD-214, along with an official document showing my time of service, medals, awards, sea time, job qualifications, schools, and training.

She took my documents and entered the information into her computer while I waited. My back hurt, but the dizziness from the chemo was clearing up, and I looked around the office to pass the time. It was small and painted gray, with pictures and posters of happy Veterans on the wall. I turned away from the photos. Most Veterans were not this happy after their time serving. Many of them came home with PTSD and a hollow feeling in their stomach that their service had been for nothing.

"Okay," Delan said, startling me out of my thoughts. "I have found you in the system. You served from September 26, 1988, until your honorable discharge on February 2, 1995. Your specialty was TM?"

"Yes," I said. "Yes, Torpedoman's Mate. My job included performing organizational and intermediate-level maintenance on tests and equipment that involved underwater ordnance and seawater systems. Uhm…often, my team and I were in charge of performing inspections and final closeout checks on weapons. We also performed preventive and corrective maintenance on hydraulic and pneumatic systems and other components associated with launching systems."

Delan smiled as I mouthed off the words, and I smiled back. "It doesn't matter how long ago you served; you never forget your training or duties."

"You haven't been active in the system for years," she stated.

"Yes," I said.

"Okay, let's see what we can do to get you re-registered." She typed for a while on her computer, and to pass the time, I counted.

"Okay," she said again, and I gave her my full attention. "I'm sorry, Mr. Proctor, but I'm going to have to put you down for minimal benefits."

"I don't understand."

"Well, for one, you haven't been in the system for a long time. And to qualify for full benefits, you have to prove that your cancer ties into something you did for the government during your time in service."

Her answer brought me completely out of my chemo fog. "I have to prove that I came in contact with something on duty that's now making me sick?"

"Basically, yes."

"And that's the only way I'm going to get help?"

"Yes."

"How am I supposed to prove that?" I asked, completely stunned. "It's been decades. Decades. I cannot possibly remember every single chemical or substance I came in contact with, and even if I could, how am I supposed to prove which one caused my cancer? That would take months! I don't have months! I don't even have days. My insurance has already cut me off.

"Mr. Proctor..."

"You have my medical records there," I said, completely flustered. "Pull them up. Maybe you can find something."

She pulled them up, but they were clean. The only times I went to the hospital were for the standard check-up.

"Maybe we can narrow it down," Delan said. "Were you part of Desert Storm during your service? Were you at war during that time?"

"No."

"Were you stationed in any of the bases where active health claims were underway?"

"No."

She sighed. "Well, in light of this information, you are only qualified for priority Group 5."

"Which means?"

"Zero percent disability for service connection."

I was too dumbfounded to speak.

Delan looked at me sympathetically and said, "I'm going to give you a number you can call because, based on everything you've told me, you don't qualify. And there's really nothing I can do to help."

I didn't qualify? I had just spent two hours in this place after a grueling chemo session to have this woman tell me I didn't qualify. So, a peaceful wartime and excellent service didn't qualify me for specialized benefits? What exactly did they want me to have done to qualify?

I got up shakily, completely furious at myself for believing the VA could help. I left in the first place because they were so bogged down in stipulations and bureaucracy that getting your benefits was near impossible. I walked out of the office to find Tony, waiting with Jackie and Monica.

"How did it go?" Monica asked

I shook my head. "Getting registered doesn't mean much. It means literally nothing, actually. I have to prove that my time in service was somehow responsible for my cancer to get specialized benefits."

Monica and Jackie's faces fell.

"I'm going to introduce you to someone else," Tony said.

"Someone who can cut through all of this and help you. You'll need to fill out some more paperwork."

"Okay," I said, but in my heart, I knew it wouldn't matter.

Tony said goodbye to us, and Jackie drove us home. We all sat in the car for a moment after she pulled into our gate, taking stock.

"This shouldn't be happening," I said. "People who are going through this, through literally the worst moment of their lives, shouldn't have to deal with a bunch of hurdles and red tape and bureaucracy. I'm sick," my voice broke. "And without my treatment, I'll die. I shouldn't have to deal with this. I shouldn't have to prove that I deserve their help. They are asking me to prove that I qualify to live. Do you realize that, Jackie? That's what they are asking me to do. To prove that I qualify to live."

That night, I went to sleep thinking there had to be another way, an easier way. Veterans who are dying shouldn't have to prove they qualify to live.

Jackie and Tony introduced me to more people in the coming weeks, and after every chemo session, I sat with them and tried to figure out a way to pay for my treatment. All I wanted to do was come home and rest, but I couldn't, and that infuriated and depressed me. The sale of my life insurance still hadn't come through, and my healthcare provider had completely shut down and wouldn't approve my payments until I paid the deductible. I had nightmares of them canceling my entire claim.

I called up a man Jackie introduced me to. His name was John. I explained everything that happened at the VA hospital, and he listened intently. When I was done, he asked, "What was your job rating?"

I explained that, making sure to emphasize the conditions I had to work around. Some of them were hazardous. He listened intently.

"Well, you need to go back and reapply," he said. "Based on what you've just told me, you should qualify and receive benefits. Your job specifications and associated hazards should qualify you."

I sighed in resignation. "That's not what they said."

"You need to prove it," he said impassively. "If you can go back and justify all the criteria they listed, they will pay for your treatment in full."

Not this again. "If I could, I would. But I can't. Also, time's not on my side. What exactly do you guys want me to write, anyway? My every sleeping and waking moment during service?"

"Not that exactly, but close enough."

"You can't be serious?"

"I'll email a link to you. Go through and answer the questions. It should help you get closer to getting your benefits."

I sighed again.

"Many Veterans give up," John said as if my sighs were an indication I was about to give up, too. "They get frustrated with the red tape and the bureaucracy, and they give up. Don't give up, Greg."

I couldn't give up if I wanted to; my life depended on it.

That night, the email with the link came. I opened it, and it was an online VA form. It asked me basic questions like what is your name? What was your job? When was your period of service? And then, finally, tell us why you believe you need to have benefits.

I took a deep breath and began typing. I wrote in detail about my time at the Navy, detailing my first moments at Boot Camp, where I was trained in physical fitness and taught about firearms, firefighting, seamanship, and damage control. I didn't forget to include the core values of teamwork and discipline I received. Done with that, I detailed my time onboard the Navy ship I served on, making sure to outline my duties and responsibilities while including the hazardous chemicals and high-voltage equipment I worked around.

Done; I reviewed the forms several times before anxiously mailing them. When they replied, it was a "No."

"Although your medical records show a diagnosis of multiple myeloma," a part of the email stated, "your service treatment records do not contain complaints, treatment, or diagnosis for this condition. We did not find a link between your medical condition and military service. (38 CFR 3.303) Service connection cannot be established.

Service connection may be granted for a disability that began in military service or was caused by some event or experience in service. (38 CFR 3.303)

Service connection for multiple myeloma cancer is denied since this condition neither occurred in nor was caused by service. (38 CFR 3.303, 38 CFR 3.304)."

I shut my laptop after reading that and went to sleep.

The next day, while Jackie drove me to chemo treatment, I told her everything that had happened. "I'm done," I said. "These people, these people they keep… I'm just done."

"They make it hard for everyone," Jackie said. "Just ask Tony. That's why he started his foundation to help Veterans because he knows how near impossible it is to get the benefits you deserve. You have to keep pushing. You can't give up."

"Look at me, Jackie. You've been driving me to chemo and back. You've been here from the beginning. You see the state I'm in. I don't want to give up, Jackie, but I'm already fighting plenty as it is. I don't want to add this to it. I only have enough energy for this cancer. I'm not going to give these people my energy if they are not going to give me anything back in return."

"What about the sale of your life insurance? How's that coming along?"

I sighed deeper. "I'm sending them another email today. I honestly don't know what the hold-up is."

"Keep the faith, Gregory. Everything will work out fine. God has got you. You know He does."

"Thanks. It's just really hard."

"I know. But it wouldn't be a battle if it was easy."

I chuckled. "No, it wouldn't."

Later that evening, I contacted the insurance policy buyer I had chosen, American Life Fund. They were the leading viatical settlement company in the United States. I got an email right back saying they could have an offer for my insurance. However, they couldn't move forward because my insurance was irrevocable, and I needed the signatures of my beneficiaries to sell. I sighed in even more frustration.

Getting Monica's and Victoria's signatures wasn't a problem. It was Gabriela who bothered me. She still hadn't reached out to me since our first call, and I wondered what she would say when she found out I was selling the policy. I loathed having to call her for something like this, but I had no choice.

But when I called, she wouldn't speak to me. I sent emails and texts explaining that I needed her signature because I was selling my life insurance and couldn't sell until I got it. I waited for days and got no reply. I began to wonder if she was screening my calls. Did she hate me so much that she wouldn't even text back? Had I been that horrible of a dad to her?

Then I got angry because I was desperate, and my own daughter wouldn't help me. Then my anger dissolved into hurt because I was desperate, not just for her signature, but for her. Yes, my bills were piling up, but I was walking into a transplant in a few months, and though I was optimistic God would see me through, there was not a hundred percent chance I would make it out. What if this was it for me and Gabriela? What if I died with my daughter hurt and angry at me?

In the end, I reached out to her mom, who reached out to her and got her to sign the policy. I mailed that to the insurance company and waited for their reply. It didn't come.

One week later, Monica and I went back to emailing and reaching out to people Jackie sent my way. I emailed my own contacts and moved from the couch to my home office desk, fighting nausea as I typed email after email, while my health provider ignored my bills as they piled high. But nothing clicked; nothing worked; they all said the same thing,

"You have to prove that you deserve benefits."

By the end of the second week, Tony sent me an email with a gift card attached to it.

"At my foundation," the email said, "we cannot give you thousands of dollars. We may not be able to give you the help that you want. But we try to help our people with whatever we can. I hope things work out as soon as possible.

Sincerely, Tony."

I opened the gift card. It contained $100 for groceries. I felt a wave of gratitude hit me. Then sadness, because I'd become someone who couldn't afford groceries.

Staying Alive

One day, at the height of COVID—restless, angry, and rapidly becoming impoverished due to lack of funds and work—I walked into my home office and looked around. My work laptop was on the table; three more were in various parts of the room, and two more were in the living room. I looked at them in surprise, as if it was somehow just hitting me that I had six laptops when I only ever used one. I went around picking them up one after the other, and when Monica walked into the living room an hour later in a messy bun, sweatshirt, and sad eyes, tethering on the edge of COVID depression that had engulfed the entire world, I said, "We are selling these."

"Good," she said and flopped on the couch. "Nobody needs six laptops."

Though we were selling because we were dangerously low on cash, it had felt free to do so, like a cleansing, as if I was somehow regaining the part of me that had thought I needed six laptops to function. When we met the guy in a deserted parking lot who bought one, wearing masks and standing more than five feet away to make sure we didn't touch, he was ecstatic. "I can't believe you have the Dell 13 laptop," he cried. "I have been looking for this!"

When we drove home afterward, I felt so good I said, "We should sell more things."

"Easy now," Monica said, laughing. "Maybe COVID will end soon, and we won't have to sell anything else. God, I really hope it ends soon," she added with a deep sigh.

COVID would last longer than we anticipated. And when my cancer came, sending me deeper into impoverishment, I sold something I thought I never would.

"Monica," I said, "I think we should open a GoFundMe page."

We were stuck in traffic. It was sweltering, and I just wanted to get back to my air-conditioned home and sleep away the chemo for the day. But this had been brewing in my mind since the insurance company dropped the deductible bomb on me. My business credit cards were masked, American Life Insurance still hadn't gotten back to me, and the Veterans hospital was a dead-end. Time was running out, and though they didn't want to, I knew the clinic would soon have no choice but to cut me off. Still, I had been hesitant at the thought of a GoFundMe page because the idea of opening one had given me the feeling of being a pauper, a feeling I had sworn never to feel again at eighteen when I walked into the Navy.

Growing up, even in the moments when we struggled, my parents held their heads high and never asked for help, not even from family, who would have been happy to. So, it surprised me when the idea of a GoFundMe page popped into my head. I wondered what my mom would think about it, and my father. I wondered what they would say if they knew I was relying on gift cards for gas and groceries.

I looked over at Monica and knew exactly what she would think. Her independent and discreet Peruvian roots would hate the idea of asking for money from people who weren't family. True to form, her sweaty brow had creased into a frown. "I don't think we should do that, Greg."

"Yes. I know you don't like …"

"I really don't. We can't ask strangers on the internet for money. How would that make us look?" Her hand clenched the steering wheel tighter. "My family will help if I ask."

"They already have. I don't think we should ask them anymore." I had my own pride, too.

Monica's family backed up their loan by calling and asking what we needed and how much more they could help. They still had the prayer circle for me going every morning. They also sent me positive words of affirmation daily. Monica's Aunt Rosa was particular about it. She had sent me one every day from the beginning of my diagnosis. Her consistency and love were heartwarming. Monica's family would give more if we asked, but I was hesitant to ask them again. They were still battling the effects of the pandemic more than we were; it would be thoughtless to ask them for more money. At least with the GoFundMe page, the only people who would give were the people who could and really wanted to. I said the same to Monica. There would be no need for this if the insurance sale had come through, but alas, we were still waiting.

"Maybe we can reach out to the insurance and ask for an update," Monica said. "You could try to log in to see if you have access to the page or something. If you don't, it would mean the sale has gone through, right?"

"Already did yesterday. No luck."

Monica sighed. "Still, we can't open a GoFundMe page. That's like telling people we are broke."

"We *are* broke. We are both out of work, we cannot afford groceries, the insurance company hasn't gotten back to us, the VA hospital is a no-go, and my chemo bills are piling up. Oncology SA could stop treatment if we don't pay soon. Dr. Rao has been very patient, but I honestly don't think we have a choice."

"So, ask your family. Or friends? Anything is better than opening a GoFundMe page."

"No."

"Why not?! How is it better to ask for money from total strangers over your family? Is this some cultural American thing?"

I fought the urge to roll my eyes. "No. I don't want to put anyone in the position to turn us down. Imagine you had asked your family for help, and they were unable to; how would that have made you feel?"

Monica went silent, and I looked out the window. Cars had begun to move slowly, but the sweltering atmosphere remained. One of the worst things about chemo was being stuck in traffic afterward. On good days, I felt dizzy and, hopefully, could fall asleep. But on bad days like today, I was restless edgy, as if my skin could no longer contain my bones.

"Fine," Monica said. "You set up the GoFundMe page, and I'll reach out to the rest of the organizations Jackie sent us and see what we can get from them."

Right, the organizations. We had applied to the first one, American Veterans Aid, and they had taken a long look at my finances and decided that I was way too rich to need assistance. My finances from the last five years before COVID showed a prosperous, bountiful income, but the COVID drought, the misfortune with the house, and Tru-Spot had cleared all of that. I had considered emailing them to explain everything: the house, Tru-Spot, my dismal lack of clients, but I stopped myself.

They had made their decision. I just needed to find some other options. I didn't blame them either. Anyone looking from outside would think I had the means to pay for my chemo. And I would if my health provider wasn't giving me the runaround. Also, they no doubt had hundreds of Veterans seeking help. It must be hard choosing who to help and who to turn down. I didn't envy that position.

The traffic finally improved, and five minutes later, we were driving at a much better pace.

"I'm sorry," I said. I wasn't sure what I was apologizing for. I just knew that I was.

Monica took my hand gently. "Nothing to be sorry about. This is where we are now. We just have to make it work."

When we got home, Monica went to prepare dinner, and I settled in front of my laptop to create the GoFundMe page. It felt surreal to be doing this. Again, I wondered what my father would say if he was here.

An hour later, I was done, and our page was live. I wondered how soon people would start to donate; I wondered if they would. I wondered if they would wonder why Gregory Proctor, of all people, was opening a GoFundMe page. I felt a trickle of shame go through me, and to distract myself, I closed the tab and switched to Facebook. I scrolled up and down, looking at posts and comments. I posted daily here, sharing my treatment updates and inspiration for people who needed it. Monica was part of many multiple myeloma groups, too. She was on them every day, checking for updates and success stories to cheer me up. But the worry about my treatment and payment had kept both of us away from my page. Monica hadn't been by in a while, and I hadn't been in almost three weeks. But now, I found myself craving support.

I went through posts, reading and leaving comments. Then I went through some of my old posts and saw new comments had come in. I clicked on them and read. A few pulled me in. One was from Wilton Guerra, a long-time Facebook friend, who said, "You got this, man! You are strong and have the mindset of a champion. No matter how hard it gets or if the battle seems lost, you know you can and will win at the end. Be strong and keep up the fight. Never give up. Remember, you rock and will continue to do so."

Another from Julia Brave said, "I admire men who cry. For me, it is normal. Men are human beings, too. I will continue praying for you. I repeat in my mind, ho'oponopono mantra, for your healing."

I quickly copied the word "ho'oponopono," and checked the meaning in a new tab. "Ho'oponopono" was a Hawaiian phrase that meant "to make things right" or "move them back to balance." It was often recited by individuals to rid themselves of the burden in order to heal. I shook my head in astonishment, moved by her words. Her comment was from a post I made after a grueling chemo day. I'd posted a picture of myself crying. I'd wanted to let them know it was okay to cry, to share your pain, especially if you'd been conditioned not to do so. I thought I'd be mocked for it, but this comment felt so heartwarming. So validating.

I scrolled further, and another comment from Roni Jones-Grant said: "Thank you for posting your journey. It has made me less anxious about a possible SCT in the future. You are such an inspiration. God bless you and your family." God bless you, too, I thought, as I liked her comment and made a mental note to message her and ask about her future SCT.

One from Brenda Chavers really floored me. "You are a true warrior, my friend," it said. "God has carried you every step of the way and given you the strength to keep fighting. And fight you will, today and every day, until complete healing has taken over your being. We are still standing in the gap with you, trusting and believing in the promises of God to all of us as children of God. God has great plans for your life. You have given the MM community so much hope and knowledge to fight this disease. Most importantly, you have allowed your faith in God to shine. God bless you, my faithful friend. Love and many prayers to you."

My heart filled with warmth and joy. Her words captured everything I'd been trying to do with my posts: give people hope and knowledge to fight this disease. Also, I was so honored she had pointed out my faith in God. It was something I was immensely proud of now. I wanted everyone to see and know it. Filled with gratitude, I messaged her immediately to thank her for her comment.

As I signed off a few minutes later, I realized pain can be very isolating, but it's self-conceited to assume you are the only one suffering. What lessens pain isn't tolerance; it is acceptance and commiseration—finding people who get it, who have experienced it, and letting their understanding or your understanding of said pain lessen theirs.

As the days progressed and our chemo bills piled up, we began to reach out to the rest of the organizations Jackie had provided us. Money was slowly trickling into the GoFundMe page, but it was nowhere close to paying for the deductible. Monica focused on that, calling and sending emails to the financial aid organizations to notify them of our plight and seek help. There were several of them, each one designed to care for cancer needs you never think about until you, well, have cancer. Needs like covering your chemo drugs prescription, associated transplant costs, or even groceries and gas.

As we scoured through these organizations, it hit me again how much I'd been living a very different reality before cancer. I never had to worry about things like this, not even when my father was sick. In many ways, it felt like I had taken my good fortune for granted like I had been living in a bubble that just had to burst. I stayed up many nights thinking about this, thinking that I had gone from someone who gave help, financially and otherwise, to someone who now needed it. It humbled and embarrassed me. It scared me, too, because I thought, what if this was it for me? What if I never made it out of this place of desperate need?

Almost all of the organizations we reached out to turned me down the moment I submitted my financials and tax records. It didn't matter that I was out of a job and rapidly running out of money. Everything on paper said I was supposed to be able to handle this myself. I was supposed to be able to afford it. Their emails seemed to say these services aren't for you. They are for people who can't put down $5,000 on a house or pay a $90,000 tax bill. It seemed as if the black cloud that was raining down on me continued to follow my path, determined to break me.

Eventually, I gave up on these organizations and sought out Veterans on Facebook groups who had been sick with cancer. I bombarded them with questions, the lead one being, how did you get the government to cover the expense of your chemo? They all pretty much told me the same thing: prove you got sick in line with something you did in service, and they will cover it.

I refreshed the GoFundMe page several times, checking the numbers, hoping and hoping they would eventually be enough to afford the deductible, but they weren't even close. It was embarrassing to go into chemo, to sit down and take drugs that I couldn't afford. I called my healthcare provider time and time again, asking if there was any way they could forfeit the deductible just for now, just until I could afford it. My bills were piling up, for God's sake! Did they not care that I could die?

I got the same canned reply, "You have to pay your deductible,

Mr. Proctor. We will cover it as soon as you pay your deductible."

I came to see the American Health Care System in a brand-new light. It had never occurred to me before how completely callous it was, how obscenely expensive. We have some of the best healthcare systems in the world, but we make patients pay through their teeth to afford it. The people who can't are denied life. It was all about the money, all about how much you could afford, never about the patient in pain or the caregiver who was overwhelmed and at their wit's end. I saw it every time I looked at Monica, every morning and night, when she pulled up my chart to check my markers, my diet, my symptoms, and my drugs. She was overloaded with stress and fear, and she couldn't stop because, for her, it wasn't even an option. She didn't sit for hours to get chemo or stay up at night because of the blinding pain from cancer, but she was in pain nonetheless; she was suffering just as much as I was.

I was afraid, but I still felt that pull, that comfort from the day I went back to church, and in the midst of my chaos, there it was like an anchor holding me down. And I held onto that every day as I went back and forth to chemo, as I called the insurance company, as I sent another email that received a rejection, as I refreshed the GoFundMe page. There it was until one day, Dr. Rao walked up to me after my chemo session. I was just standing up.

"Mr. Proctor, can I talk to you?"

I started before she could, cringing with every word I said. "Dr. Rao, I know my insurance company has been giving you the runaround, but I promise we are doing everything we can to speed up the process."

"Yes, that's what I want to talk to you about."

"That's what I'm saying …"

"Mr. Proctor?"

"Yes," I said and went silent.

"You don't have to worry about that anymore."

"Excuse me?"

"Well, we didn't want to tell you in case it didn't pan out, but we submitted your name for consideration in the LLS community and told them about your deductible, and they have agreed to cover it. Your insurance will get the money next week."

"The LLS community?"

"Yes, The Leukemia, Lymphoma Society. They are a charitable organization dedicated to fighting cancer like yours. We have a great relationship with them, and many of our patients have benefitted from their generosity. They will take care of your deductible; don't worry about it."

"Are you… are you serious?"

"Yes, you don't have to worry about the bills anymore. They've been taken care of."

I stood there staring at her, completely dumbfounded. "Oh my God. I don't even. How did you, when did you…? We needed this. How did you know we needed this?"

Dr. Rao smiled warmly. "Not all patients who come for chemo are prepared for the financial burden, even the ones who think they are. So, we do our best to help in any way we can."

My eyes watered. "Thank you so much."

That night, I went home, and for the first time in weeks, I slept like a baby. The next morning, when I woke up, I knew exactly what I had to do.

"I'm going to sell my coin collection," I said to Monica.

She looked at me in shock. "But you love it."

I did. I never thought I'd sell them. They were gold, silver, and platinum coins I'd gathered at different and significant moments of my life. I loved them so much I barely touched them, treating them like a prize in a display room. But that morning, I went and looked at them, and I saw they were just coins. I had treated them with so much reverence, like this invaluable thing I couldn't live without, much like the laptops and my work. I had treated these things more importantly than I treated myself and, often, the people around me.

And now, they were just things, things that I could die without, things that didn't mean as much to me in light of cancer and chemo. So, I put them on the market, and a week later, they were snatched up for forty percent less than I thought they would bring. The dealer was shrewd and out to make as much profit as possible, and for a moment, the old me, the me who cared about winning and putting people in their place and being right, came out.

"You can't be serious," I said. "This collection is rare. Very rare."

But clarity dawned even more as I repeated myself. So, my intentions morphed from making the best deal to freeing myself. And as I signed the papers to transfer ownership, I said to myself, they are just things, just things.

And all the real things, all the important things—you can never buy or sell them.

Being healthy in mind and body is a priceless, incredible gift. Ironically, we take it for granted and treat it as an afterthought because many of us do not fully grasp what it means to have our body or mind shut down. So, we work until we are burnt out, foregoing breaks and sleep or good food in favor of the next big project. We ply our bodies with greasy food and alcohol, nicotine, and sugar, taking pleasure from things that kill us. Though I had spent most of my life living right, I hadn't done it because I understood the true worth of health; I did it because I was afraid of death because I wanted to be one of the few men in my family to cross the sixty-five-years threshold. So, when I fell sick after having done everything right, I felt betrayed by my body. Until I realized that being healthy isn't just about staying alive; it's about living and participating in moments, being present in all of them, cherishing and appreciating them. And many of us never do this until we see our time start to run out.

In truth, none of us actually have our own time, but we do have moments. Heck, we have the chance and grace to create them ourselves. Why do we never create them? Why do we wait and postpone and ignore? Why do we act like we have all the time in the world when we don't? Why do we lose opportunities to create moments?

With the deductible handled by the LLS Copay Assistance Program, I focused on getting better and being in the moment. I looked at Monica with more warmth and held her hand longer. I smiled when she put the bland rice and chicken in front of me or when she came to inform me of this or that in my health charts. I settled in to read books, taking my time to enjoy them and connect with them. I created posts for my social media pages, drawing inspiration from mundane things like my daily walks with Monica through the trails or even how blue the sky seemed today. I lingered on these walks, stared at the trees, looked at the wildlife, and breathed in the fresh air devoid of car smoke. I took pictures with Monica at every turn, capturing her smile as we walked the trails together, the light that was returning to her eyes, or the bounce of her ponytail as she walked. I called my mom on the phone and spoke with her longer. I spoke to my siblings too, my brother and his wife, Robert, and longtime dear friend Wayne, who, like Robert, had driven all the way from Washington to see me and cheer me up. Every interaction and every action was a chance for me to make a moment out of it, and I did.

I went to church every Sunday, asking Pastor Brazil what I could do to help and how I could contribute or be of service. I read my Bible every day, marveling at how God seemed to have a story or verse for everything. It stunned me that I had lived my life without these words to guide and comfort me; I couldn't get enough of them now. I went through my podcast episodes and paused in shock when I realized two guests had experienced cancer. One of them was Bari Ross; she had battled head and neck cancer for years, and the other was Saz, the artist whose mother died from multiple myeloma. I realized then it was why the words had sounded vaguely familiar to me when I heard them after my MRI. Somehow, these podcasts with these guests felt like foreshadowing. I wondered if God was trying to tell me something then. Had He been trying to tell me something all my life, and I'd just been too self-absorbed to see it?

The months passed, and I got stronger, settling into a less painful routine. My chemo sessions were reduced from five days a week to three. And they no longer left me depleted and woozy. Also, because of the effects of one of my chemo drugs, I began wolfing down two plates of food in one sitting—food with a better taste that made me almost cry with joy and relief. You never fully appreciate the pleasure of food until you have to live without the best parts of it. I enjoyed every morsel and bite put in front of me. Before long, I had gained several pounds, and Monica chuckled with pleasure as she poked my belly. To combat that, I took longer walks. We laughed more now, her sacrifice and care of me making me love her deeper than I thought possible.

When my birthday came a few months later, on September 15th, I woke up to Monica's smiling face hovering over mine.

"Happy birthday, Mi Amor," she said.

I smiled right back. I had just turned fifty-one. It had seemed impossible when I first got my diagnosis; my mind and fear had convinced me I wouldn't last a month. Yet here I was, three months into chemo, feeling much better and celebrating a new age with my wife. Monica had a hearty breakfast and sugar-free cake waiting for me, and I ate them with gusto. Afterward, she settled in front of her laptop to work while I took calls and text messages from friends and family. We were going for a birthday lunch later. My mom called to deliver a heartfelt prayer; my ex-wife called, too, to ask how I was doing and how treatment was going. Robert called, and we spent an hour talking on the phone.

"Bet you didn't think you'd turn fifty-one," he said with a chuckle.

I chuckled back. "I won't lie. It was scary for a moment there."

"Well, here's to you getting so old your teeth fall out."

I laughed till my eyes watered. "Thanks, man."

I went on social media and saw my network had made birthday posts about me. My heart warmed at their thoughtful messages, and I spent the day in a state of euphoria.

Later in the evening, I coaxed Monica away from her laptop. "I'm just checking your schedule and vitals," she said. "You know Dr. Rao says—"

"Let's watch a movie," I said, cutting her off. "Take a break with me. I'll still have multiple myeloma tomorrow."

I said the same thing to her when her birthday came a week later. We went out again for food, drinks, and cake and spent the rest of the day enjoying each other's company.

A month later, at the clinic with Dr. Rao, we both got the best birthday present. "We are done with phase one," Dr. Rao said with a big smile.

"What do you mean?" Monica asked.

Her smile widened even more. "Mr. Proctor has achieved remission."

The Turning Point

After the VA denied my claim, I wanted nothing else to do with them. I never thought I would need their help, so being denied after needing it hurt my ego. I sulked for weeks, complaining to anyone who would listen how awfully I'd been treated by the Veterans Hospital. Their stipulations made no sense to me. I was a veteran; I had served my country; that should accord me the damn right to live now that I was dying. I shouldn't have to beg for their help. But deep down, I knew it wasn't about their stipulations and the fact their rules said I wasn't qualified for benefits because those rules had been in place for decades, and they weren't simply going to change it for one veteran. It had simply felt like they were telling me I wasn't good enough to live. And the fact that my healthcare provider was finally making good on their claim further bolstered my decision.

But one day, as I talked to my brother Jason on the phone, giving him updates about my chemo and treatment progression, he said, "I think you should go back to the VA."

"Nah, man," I said. "I'm done with that. They have nothing to offer me."

"Listen," he said, "you haven't been in the system since you left the Navy. So, is it so strange they would deny you benefits? You haven't been on their radar, and there are hundreds of Veterans who have been and still get denied every day for one reason or another. You should go back. At the very least, you will get the benefits you do qualify for, and who knows what could happen?"

I listened quietly as he spoke, and it occurred to me he was right. It was arrogant to simply walk in there after years of ignoring my benefits and acting like I didn't need them, just to say hey, it turns out I need you after all. The thing was, I had spent my life looking down on a lot of things and people—people who were not as intellectual as I was, not as driven, ambitious, or even wealthy. It was ironic because

I didn't come from wealth, and perhaps fighting for everything I'd earned made me resent people who didn't or people I'd seen as too lazy to fight.

If I hadn't fallen sick, I would never have walked into Faith Temple Church. It was such a small, unnoticeable retail building at the side of the crossroad, filled with kind-hearted people, that reminded me of the struggles of some of our notable Black communities. I would have been quite content to drive past it for the rest of my life. I wouldn't have volunteered my time or resources to them; I'd simply have donated and moved on to something more important, something more tasking, something that required work and skill and no heart. Because those were the things I'd become great at over the years. They just weren't the things that made me great. Now, my ego was being restrained by a higher power, and the relevance of what I had been escaping from in my previous life was now staring me in the face. Thankfully, I was now transformed to a point where I couldn't say no.

A month after speaking with my brother and being denied benefits, I scheduled a routine doctor's visit at the VA hospital. All I wanted at that point was to be on their radar. I didn't think they would change their mind about the benefits; their denial had seemed final.

On the day of my visit, with Monica by my side, I walked humbly into the hospital and waited my turn to see the doctor. After waiting for almost half an hour, we were shown into the doctor's office. We met a stately-looking doctor named Dr. Chung. He looked at my file in front of him; it was practically empty.

"Mr. Proctor," he said. "You don't have many records with the VA hospital."

I nodded. "This is my first visit in decades. I haven't used my benefits since I left the Navy in 1995."

"Why's that?" he asked.

"I never thought I would need it."

He chuckled at the irony. "So you are here for a routine checkup, then?"

"Yeah," I nodded, chuckling back. The irony wasn't lost on me.

"And he's been diagnosed with multiple myeloma," Monica added.

"Wow, that's a big one," Dr. Chung said. "Is the VA covering your expenses?

"Actually, he's been denied," Monica added.

"Denied?"

"Yeah," I added tiredly. "I'll be needing a transplant, too."

Dr. Chung stood in thought for a moment. "Alright," he said. "You did come in for a routine check-up. So I'm going to need to do an evaluation on you."

"Of course," I said.

Monica gave me a kiss and walked out of the room.

Just as Dr. Chung said, the check-up was pretty routine, except that he did it with the knowledge of my already existing multiple myeloma. When he was done, he wrote something on a piece of paper and handed it to me. I could barely read the scribble.

"I'm going to make an appointment for you at the Hematology Department," he said. "There should be an opening for you in a few weeks. I think you should get tested for multiple myeloma here. We will communicate the date to you. Don't miss it."

I thought about my chemo and how awful I felt afterward. There was no doubt this appointment would fall on a chemo-treatment day. Still, I made up my mind right there to come for every VA appointment.

"I wouldn't miss it, doctor," I said.

During my chemo treatments, I often visited with other patients and caregivers via the Facebook Multiple Myeloma chat groups to stay informed and encourage each other. It was also where we announced deaths and remissions. Three months into my chemo, we had a death announcement. I didn't know the person, but the news still shocked me. It was hard to hear someone I'd likely shared the same disease or treatment regime with had died. On my way back from chemo, I talked about it to Monica. She listened quietly, and in the end, she said softly, "I know you are afraid, but there are many more that survive, and you will be one of them."

By our second VA visit, I was feeling more optimistic. This time, we met Dr. Dacus. Her smile immediately reminded me of Dr. Rao, and I relaxed in her presence. She sat us down, took my file, and began to go over it more thoroughly than Dr. Chung had. By now, I had been going through chemo for twelve weeks, and I wondered what she would find. Instead, she asked, "How's the chemo going?"

"You know how it is," I said.

"Actually, I don't," she said and laughed. "I've never had multiple myeloma, you see."

I chuckled. I definitely liked this doctor. "Well, I'd say it's a step-by-step process. Some days, I think I've mastered the symptoms; other days, I come home feeling like it's the first day all over again. I had to deal with some insurance issues in the beginning, and the stress from that didn't help my situation. But it's all being sorted out now."

"I see here that you are scheduled for a transplant next year."

I inhaled deeply and nodded. Thinking about the transplant always made me anxious. There was so much to consider. So much that could go wrong. "Yeah, that's the final stage of my treatment."

"And the VA isn't covering any of this?" she asked.

I shrugged. "I don't qualify for that extent of care."

"Hmmm. Well, I'm going to introduce you to someone who I think can help."

"Help? Like with my benefits?"

"Yes. There is a whole process involved, but if you are up for it, it could lead somewhere."

I thought about it. By this point, I honestly didn't have anything to lose. They could either agree to cover it or they wouldn't. Either way, my healthcare provider was already handling it. I at least had that, so this wasn't a do-or-die.

"Set it up," I said.

"Oh, no need to set anything up; Dr. Haile is right down the hall. Wait right here."

A few minutes later, Dr. Haile walked in with Dr. Dacus. He was tall and slim with an athletic build, gray hair, and kind eyes. More and more, I was getting surprised by the doctors of the VA hospital. So far, they were all empathetic and friendly. I wasn't sure what I'd expected, but based on the original denial I'd gotten, I wasn't expecting them to be this friendly. Dr. Haile shook my hand warmly and picked up my file. He quickly went through it with his brow furrowed and lips pursed. After a few minutes, he cleared his throat and said, "It's certainly possible for the VA to help."

"Really?" Monica asked. She had kept quiet the entire time. I figured she was going through my schedule and charts in her head.

"Absolutely," Dr. Haile said. "You would just need to go through all the series of tests that concluded you had multiple myeloma, and after that, we will submit your records for review."

"That's wonderful!" Monica said delightedly. But all I could think about was the horror of the tests I'd had to endure the first time. There was nothing "just" about them. They had been excruciatingly painful.

"Dr. Haile, couldn't you just request my records from my oncologist? I'm sure she would be happy to send them over."

"Okay, maybe I was a tad too optimistic the first time. Getting your benefits from the VA is a long shot. And they are certainly not going to hand you benefits based on another doctor's diagnosis of you. They need a diagnosis here from our doctors to prove you really do have cancer. And after that, we will send the results and your other medical records to the board for review."

"How long does the review take?"

It could be weeks or months. There's honestly no telling."

"So, this is based on a maybe? But I need to do these tests to even consider being reviewed, and even then, I could be denied."

"Yes. But we intend to follow this up on your behalf."

"Why?" I asked.

He shrugged, perplexing me even further. This was my first time meeting him. He didn't know me, and from what I could see, neither he nor Dr. Dacus had a stake in my getting better or not.

"However," he added. "If we do cover you, your location options for having the stem-cell transplant would fall in either Seattle, Washington, or Knoxville, Tennessee. Our VA transplant center in San Antonio currently doesn't have a transplant doctor who could see your case."

I began to shake my head immediately; there was no way that would work. "We have no family outside of San Antonio, and you know we have to be as close to home as possible after the transplant. We will not be able to afford the additional cost that comes with relocating and finding an apartment where I can recuperate for the next few months."

He shrugged again, "I'm sorry, but that's really how it works."

As Monica and I drove home, I considered the pros and cons. "I don't know if I can go through those tests again."

"You have to if you want to get those benefits."

"Yes, but our healthcare provider is already covering that. I'm not exactly sure why I need the VA anymore. Plus, we cannot have the transplant outside of San Antonio. There's so much to consider, and there's no way we'd be able to afford that."

"You never know," Monica said. "Just do it."

And she was right, I didn't know.

I went back in and did all the bloodwork, x-rays, scans, and physical and mental testing. And just like the first time, the poking and prodding was overwhelming, even more so now that I was going through chemo. I went back home afterward, wondering if I had done all of it for nothing. They could still deny me, and even if they didn't, my healthcare provider was already covering my chemo and would cover my transplant. I kept thinking that I didn't need them, but for some reason, and with Monica's urging, I kept following up with them, providing every record they needed, staying in touch with the doctors, and going for routine check-ups. All of it seemed redundant until it wasn't. Because, as Monica had pointed out, we never knew.

For my transplant, Dr. Rao passed me off to her transplant colleague at the Methodist Hospital BMT clinic, Dr. Cruz. Before we got there, Dr. Rao scheduled our appointment and emphasized that Dr. Cruz would be handling my care through the Stem Cell Transfer (SCT) process.

"You will not need a donor," she reiterated. "I know you will have a lot of questions," she added. "Dr. Cruz will be happy to answer them."

Upon our arrival, Dr. Cruz, a man of about five feet, firm build and low-cut blond hair, brought us back to an examining room. He reminded me of an Admiral in the Navy. In the examination room, we met one other doctor, a nurse, and a social worker. I raised my brow curiously. Was this the number of people it took to answer questions about a transplant?

"I'll leave you to it," Dr. Cruz said and walked out.

That left me even more puzzled. He wasn't going to stay? To put us at ease, the social worker-led with a smile. We exchanged pleasantries, and for the next five hours, they lectured us about stem cell transplants.

"Essentially," the nurse continued after an already lengthy lecture about SCT, "we will kill your immune system with a high dose of Melphalan, and then you'll have a day of rest, followed by the stem-cell transplant procedure."

"If the chemo treatment has worked so well, why do we still need the transplant?" Monica asked.

"Your case is considered high risk," the doctor answered, while the nurse nodded gravely in agreement. "Especially with the IGA Kappa, P-17 deletion, and sub-mutated genes. Your best course of action for potential long-term survivorship is having the transplant."

"To be honest," the doctor continued, "If Mr. Proctor was older, we probably wouldn't do a stem-cell transplant. It is very challenging for the patient, especially in the aftermath. Before the transplant, a large dose of chemotherapy will be inserted into your bloodstream. It will kill all the unhealthy cancer cells, but it will also kill the healthy ones. So, your body will be completely exposed. I'm talking absolutely vulnerable; you could die from catching a cold. That's why it's very important for the patient to be younger and in good health. It gives your body a better chance of survival and recovery."

"And these stem cells, we are getting them from his body, right?" Monica asked.

"Yes," the doctor said with a smile.

I smiled, too. Dr. Rao briefed us on this.

"The kind of transplant we are doing on you is called an autologous stem-cell transplant. You don't need a donor."

When Dr. Rao had first told me about the transplant, I immediately thought of my daughters; would they need to donate? I didn't want to put them in that situation, a place where they had to choose between my life and theirs, because what if complications arose and something awful happened to them? I concluded that if I needed a donor, I would wait on the donor's list. It never crossed my mind to ask them. It felt like such a huge thing for a father to ask his children, and as far as I was concerned, it was supposed to be the other way around.

To hear this doctor further confirm it was a blessing. I felt lucky and grateful. Also, it was amazing to think that the body that had betrayed me was now the thing that would save me.

"There are two types of bone marrow transplant," the doctor continued. "Autologous and allogeneic. An autologous bone marrow transplant, the one to be performed on you, is the kind where stem cells would be removed from your body, stored in a freezer, and then put back in your body after a large dose of chemo or radiation has killed off the toxic stem cells. In your case, we plan to harvest at least four-to-six million healthy stem cells. Typically, the average number of stem cells needed for a single transplant is two to three million. But, we are taking this much for the primary SCT and a backup if the need arises."

Monica and I sighed simultaneously, and the doctor smiled with understanding. "We hope the need doesn't arise, but those extra cells are a necessary precaution. Please," he added, "try not to worry."

"Okay," Monica said, taking my hand.

The doctor continued. "The first transplant, your transplant, is what we like to call a rescue transplant."

Rescue transplant? I liked that.

"The second type is the allogeneic bone marrow transplant. This is the type you would have needed a donor for. Someone that matches your DNA, like your children or siblings."

Monica nodded as he talked, and I realized that if it had come to that, my siblings would have been happy to donate to me. I wondered what I would have said if they offered. I was glad to never find out. In this type of transplant, you could also get from a donor who wasn't related to you, and even then, finding a match or a partial match wasn't easy. I thought of all the people who had no friends or families, people who had been waiting for years on the donor's list, and I felt sick to my stomach. The fact that I had a ton of options and was contemplating not even using them made me feel worse. There were people who didn't have the good fortune I did.

I wondered if, with my own condition, I would ever be able to donate to them if they ever needed it. I wondered if I could ask the doctors to take as many stem cells as they needed in case my daughters needed it in the future. I was still worried about them getting multiple myeloma.

"Now, after the transplant," the nurse said, "comes engraftment syndrome."

"Engraftment syndrome?" I asked.

"Yes, it's part of the transplanted process where your body accepts the transplanted cells and begins making new blood cells. Now, engraftment syndrome is the reaction that occurs while your body does this. We don't fully understand why this happens, but we can attribute it to your cells getting reacclimated again. Often, engraftment syndrome can lead your body to go through fever, anemia, bleeding, likely damage to your organs, and dietary problems."

"Wow," Monica said.

"Don't be alarmed," said the nurse. "We will be right there the entire time. We will take your temperature every day and run daily blood tests. And, of course, we will monitor you for diarrhea, vomiting, and other complications."

"How long is the engraftment syndrome supposed to last?" I asked.

"One to two weeks."

"Wow," Monica said again.

"And you will need to stay very close to the transplant center in case of complications," the doctor said. "We need to be able to have you back in immediately in case anything goes wrong."

"Like what?"

"For one, the transplant could fail."

I swallowed nervously.

"But don't worry," the nurse said. "We will keep you for observation for as long as needed. Once we check and make sure you've not had a fever for forty-eight hours, you are able to eat, your side effects have become controlled with medicine, you have safe levels of blood cell counts, and you have someone at home to watch you closely, then we will send you home."

The social worker was up next. She adjusted her round-rimmed glasses and opened her file.

"Mr. Proctor," she said, "it will take you at least a full year to recover. In that time, you could be ill for months, and your mental and emotional health could be unstable. You could also experience long periods of depression, anxiety, and anger.

"Wow," Monica said.

"It's important that you have a strong support system."

I looked at Monica with gratitude and smiled.

"And," the social worker continued, "that your finances are in order because you will not be able to work during this period. Do you have that, Mr. Proctor?"

I thought about the sale of my insurance. The American Life Fund still hadn't gotten back to me, but I was hopeful they would before the transplant.

"Yes, we do," I said confidently.

The social worker nodded in approval. "Good. A transplant is no small feat," she added. "Without resources and strong support, it can be traumatic. I hope everything works out for you."

"Thank you," I said.

"Do you have any more questions?" the doctor asked.

I thought for a moment and looked at Monica, who shook her head. "Not right now," I responded.

After, Dr. Cruz returned and asked if the discussion had addressed our questions and concerns. Monica and I were so overwhelmed with the extensive amount of materials and possible side effects that we simply nodded. However, despite the situation and the fact the stem-cell transplant felt like a mad scientist project, we both felt comfortable with Dr. Cruz.

I went home and did my own research, reading article after article until my eyes were sore. Afterward, I shut off my computer and thought about calling my daughters. I tried to keep them in the loop as the transplant drew closer, but Gabriela had completely shut me out, and only Victoria took time out of her busy schedule to reply to my messages or call me back. I did my best to be okay with that, to be more understanding of their feelings and decisions about me, but it hurt all the same. It hurt to be shut out like that.

Listening to my call to Gabriela go to voicemail for the third time, I sighed, took off my glasses, rubbed my eyes, and settled into sleep. When I woke, the email from my primary healthcare provider was waiting for me. They stated quite simply I had reached my limit and they would not be covering any more medical expenses after my transplant. Whatever else happened then, I was on my own.

I tried not to panic as I read the email, but I did. My hands shook as I refreshed the email over and over to see if they had sent another one to counter the first. But there was none. They couldn't be done after the transplant; it may have been the end of my chemo treatment, but it was the beginning of another journey. I needed after-stem-cell transplant care, or I could die.

Monica walked into the room carrying a laundry basket, and I called her over to read the email. She read, set the basket down, and sighed. "What are we going to do?" she asked.

I was already dialing the number of my healthcare provider. A nurse care manager named Steve picked up. I went straight to the point. "I just received an email stating that I'm at my limit."

"Okay."

"It states here that I won't be liable for coverage after my transplant. How is that possible?"

"Well, Mr. Proctor, it's like the email said. You are already at your limit. We will cover the transplant and all the bills that come with it, but we cannot go past that."

They couldn't be serious. "Do you understand what happens after a transplant?" I asked. "Especially one involving cancer? I'll need to be on maintenance drugs, labs, and numerous follow-up tests. I will need months to adjust, and working will completely be out of the question. What if I relapse? What if something goes wrong, and I need to go back to the hospital? Then what?"

"Mr. Proctor," Steve said. "We have honestly done all that we can for you. If we could cover your transplant, we would, but it's like you said, transplant patients need a lot of aftercare, and based on your limit, we just cannot cover that."

In the days that followed, I was furious with myself, angry for believing my primary healthcare provider would actually come through for me. I had spent weeks trying to get them to cover my chemo-treatment cost. Why did I believe they would stick to it?

"At least we still have the VA hospital," Monica said earnestly. "We need to keep in touch more than ever now. We have to follow up. We cannot afford to lose coverage after your transplant. We can't."

My nights became sleepless. I tossed and turned, thinking of all the implications of not having coverage after the transplant. Monica was right. I wouldn't be able to work for at least a year, and neither would she because she would spend it taking care of me. If the insurance company wasn't going to cover it, then I needed to find a way. One particular night, unable to sleep, I stayed up checking to see if the sale of my life insurance had come through. It had been months now. What was the holdup? I sent them another email.

Beyond thankful I had stuck with the VA, I called Dr. Haile to find out how the review was going.

"My insurance company will not cover my post-transplant care and maintenance," I said. "I need this to work more than ever."

"I understand, Mr. Proctor," he said. "But don't worry. Your review is underway, and I'll let you know as soon as anything changes."

A month passed two, and I heard nothing back, whether from the American Life Fund or Dr. Haile. My mind was clouded with worry and fear. To distract me, Monica signed us up for Jackie's Christmas toy drive— Making Spirits Bright. Monica's sister, Pamela, was in town visiting us, and she joined us, too. On that cold December morning, all of us huddled in the car and, with the money Jackie raised at the foundation, went to buy toys for kids whose parents couldn't afford to play Santa for them. My mind cleared, and my worries dissolved as I picked out toys I hoped the kids would like.

Monica and I had considered having kids before the cancer. We had talked about it extensively. I already had two daughters and wasn't exactly keen on having more kids, but I knew how important it was for Monica to have a child. And I thought too that perhaps it wouldn't hurt to try again, to do the fatherhood thing right this time. We ended up buying toys for five hundred kids. As we packaged them in fancy Christmas wrappers, I wondered what it would feel like to adopt a kid, to give them a proper home, or at least the home Monica and I shared.

We drove to the church and spent several hours laughing, playing, and wrapping the toys for the next day's toy drive. We didn't get to see the children the following day, as I realized it was in my best interest not to get sick prior to my upcoming procedure. I'd hoped to be there to see their faces light up. However, I settled for my imagination. Just knowing all of our efforts would bring joy to kids and a sense of peace to the parents who couldn't afford to purchase any toys further eased my mind.

That night, as we prepared for bed, I had the sudden urge to check my email.

"Leave it," Monica said. "You'd just had a good day. Don't ruin that by worrying."

"I won't," I said as I turned the laptop on.

"Greg?"

"Fine," I said and backed away from the computer. I went to bed, and with Monica snuggled close to me, I fell asleep.

The next morning, I woke up, prayed, had my breakfast, and then checked my email. There was one from American Life Funds. My hands shook nervously as I opened it. We got an offer for $85k. I gasped when I saw it; I wasn't sure whether it was in relief or shock. My life insurance was originally valued at $400k. The cost of the aftercare would far exceed $85k, and this wasn't accounting for things that could go wrong. It wouldn't be enough to keep us fed and alive for the next year. Nevertheless, I breathed a deep sigh and emailed them to let them know I would take it. That night before I slept, I went on my knees and told God that I'd done everything I could. It was up to Him now.

Toward the end of the same week, the VA reached out to let us know they would cover every dime of the stem-cell transplant and my post-maintenance care for up to two years. And, the email continued, they had worked it out so I could have the transplant here in San Antonio. Monica and I cried with relief.

I still think back to reading that email, to the joy and relief that flooded my heart. Some part of me had been worried about the transplant, anxious about all the things that could go wrong, but after I saw that email, my worries ceased. I knew God had it all under control.

Rebirth

Two weeks before my transplant, I was anxious. I walked around the house jittery, jumping at random sounds. I lost sleep and my appetite for food, which was ironic because I was eating tastier meals now. To calm my nerves and rejuvenate my mind, Monica and I went on more walks on the trails and did more research on the transplant and stem-cell collection. And to calm my mind even further, I prayed and read my bible more.

My social media DMs and emails were blowing up with goodwill and motivational messages from friends, family, colleagues, and strangers who knew about my stem-cell transplant. My mom called; my siblings, too. Monica's twin sister and their Aunt Rosa sent encouraging text messages and prayers—each one more fervent and heartfelt than the last. Their words and prayers strengthened me, gave me courage, and rejuvenated my faith. Because of them, I fully comprehended the value of having friends and family rooting and praying for you.

I tried not to worry about all the things that could go wrong, but it was hard not to. It felt like my body was about to get stripped down and put back together again. I wondered what that would feel like; I wondered what the other side would look like. But every time my worries tried to weigh me down, I'd think of the prayers over me and feel comforted. The support and love I got were like the sun peeking through the clouds on a cold day.

The week of my stem-cell collection began with the insertion of a Quinton catheter in my chest. That day, the morning dawned cold and frosty. I dressed for comfort, wearing black sweatpants and a gray polo sweater. Monica wore jeans and a thick sweater with a pair of glasses. Her eyes looked tired that morning, as though she'd barely slept the night before. I figured she wore glasses to prevent people from asking or staring too long at her eyes.

With Monica driving, we got to the hospital at eight a.m. To prepare for the transplant, my doctors had spent the last few days pumping me with a drug called GRANIX. Before that, my transplant had been validated by another bone marrow biopsy.

To take my mind off the stem-cell transplant, I resorted to focusing on the process rather than the outcome. "What's the drug for?" I asked as they ministered it to me.

"It's to stimulate your stem cells by bringing them from your bone marrow into your bloodstream."

"And then what happens next?"

"Well, typically, we aim to collect enough stem cells for two transplants."

Of course. Dr. Cruz had explained to me that—in the event the first transplant failed—we would need a second one. I was very anxious about that, too. I had no desire to go through this again; once was enough for a lifetime.

The nurse continued. "On average, we need two million stem cells, three at the most for a transplant. So, we need your body to give us a minimum of four million stem cells or a maximum of six."

"That's a lot," I said, chuckling.

"It is." The nurse chuckled, too. "But your body is good for it. That's the amazing thing about the human body."

It truly was.

To get the catheter inserted, I sat, anxiously waiting for the surgeon to come begin the procedure. We were actually early, and the doctor showed up on time, fifteen minutes later.

"Okay, Mr. Proctor," he said, walking in. "Let's get you started."

The nurse rolled me into the surgical room. After being placed into the proper position on the surgery table, the anesthesiologist said, "Mr. Proctor, we are going to sedate you, and then the doctor will come in with his assistants and begin the surgery process."

"Okay," I said. I sat still as the anesthesiologist began the sedation. Done with that, she left, and the doctor came in and began a search for a vein in my upper chest area. When he couldn't find a suitable one, he went for my neck. A few minutes later, the anesthesia kicked in, and I was knocked out cold. When I came an hour later, I tried not to squirm, but it was hard. The sensation from the operation was like that of a sharp straw digging into my chest. It was very uncomfortable.

"Try not to touch it," the surgeon said.

You try not to touch it, I wanted to say back. I wondered how he would feel if he had someone digging a straw into his neck. I sat still for a minute, feeling weird and self-conscious to have the catheter sticking into my jugular vein. It was the same side as where the mating port had been implanted into my chest, but it hadn't hurt this much. I decided to shake it off.

But the pain from the catheter was mild at first until it slowly crept up to the point where I couldn't move my neck sideways. I felt an overwhelming irritation and the urge to dig into my neck and pull out the catheter.

"Are you alright?" Monica asked.

"No," I snapped in irritation.

A nurse wheeled in a wheelchair and directed me to sit in it. We were to go home and return the next day for the stem-cell collection. My neck was stiffened; I stood up awkwardly and sat in the wheelchair. The nurse wheeled me out while Monica followed by my side, checking her phone. The pain increased the farther we went, and by the time we got to the exit, I was in so much pain.

"This isn't our exit," Monica said when we got there. Embarrassed, the nurse began to turn the wheelchair, and I sighed in disgust and exasperation. We finally got to the right exit, and Monica helped me into the car, got into the driver's side, and said, "We are stopping to pick up lunch at the restaurant on the way home."

"Why?" I snapped.

"Don't you want lunch?" she asked in surprise.

I sighed. "Yes, I do."

"Are you alright?" she asked again.

"This catheter hurts like hell."

"Sorry," she said as she drove out of the parking lot. "I'm sure it will be better in a few hours."

But all I could think of was the pain at the moment and how it seemed to be reaching an unbearable intensity. Monica hadn't been driving for long when I snapped again. "Stop driving so close to the sidewalk!"

"I'm not!" Monica snapped back, embarrassed. Driving on the roads of San Antonio made her anxious, and she hated it when I criticized her driving. But the more she drove, the more I found fault. By the time we got to the restaurant to pick up food, she'd had enough.

"If you don't stop raising your voice at me," she said, crying, "I'll park the car and get an Uber. Is that what you want?!"

Ashamed of my behavior, I said nothing. By the time we got home, she wasn't speaking to me. She headed straight for the bedroom, and I went into the bathroom to take a look at the catheter. Was it supposed to hurt this much? I got there, stood in front of the mirror, and a few minutes later, a tremendous amount of blood started to spread all over my gray polo shirt.

"Monicacaaaaaaaaa!" I screamed.

She ran into the bathroom in a panic and screamed right back when she saw the blood.

"We have to get you back to the hospital!"

Slowly, she guided me out of the bathroom, down the stairs, and into the car. I didn't care how she drove this time; I just wanted to get to the Stone Oak Methodist Hospital as quickly as possible.

By the time we got there, the ER representative took one look at me and rushed me into the emergency room. There, the male doctor had me pull off my polo shirt and saw the original surgeon hadn't properly stitched me up.

"Don't worry, Mr. Proctor," he said when he saw the anxiousness in my face. "I'll have you stitched up in no time."

As he did, I explained I was a multiple myeloma patient who was getting prepared for stem-cell collection the very next day. On hearing that, the doctor decided it was best to reach out to my transplant doctor that evening due to the severity of the large amount of blood lost. They went back and forth, and several hours later, my doctor and the surgeon agreed the doctor would stitch me up, and I would return to do the stem-cell collection appointment early the next morning.

The doctor stitched my neck up with only local anesthesia, which didn't numb the pain enough, and by the time we got home, I collapsed in exhaustion. As I dozed off, I thought again about how fortunate we were to have the transplant at home in San Antonio.

The next day, I went back to have the stem cells collected. I'd read up on the procedure, too, and compared to having a bone marrow biopsy, this was a cakewalk. Through the catheter, blood—in this case, large volumes of it—was collected. From it, the stem cells were extracted and returned back to my bloodstream. All of this was done by a machine specially designed for it, an apheresis machine. Blood flowed from my vein through the catheter into the machine, which then separated the stem cells from the blood and sent the blood back into my body.

I watched in fascination as my blood went through a pipe to be sieved for stem cells. The limits and wonder of modern medicine are only obvious when you are in a position to appreciate the advancement or bemoan the limitations. I appreciated the fact the machine could do something so extraordinary and bemoaned the fact I had to sit down for four hours so the machine could do its extraordinary thing. Four hours later, the doctor declared that instead of six, we had collected eight million stem cells.

"That's amazing, Mr. Proctor!" he said. "Just amazing!"

In the days leading to my stem-cell transplant, I thought about God a lot. I thought about my chemo journey through the last seven months, and I thought about the last fifty-one years of my life. I saw how God had woven and orchestrated every moment, bringing me to this point where I would so desperately need Him. The old me would have been furious at this realization at the thought that my life was controlled by anyone other than me. But the new me—the me that had been through fire and was humbled by it— saw how God had planted trees in my life and taught me to draw from the strength of my roots. I had always had the option to lean on others when I could no longer stand, to lean on God. I just never took that option because I had accepted that it was better to stand on my own.

Five days before the transplant, the hospital decided to move the procedure to another date. COVID was still in the swing, and they didn't want to endanger me by proceeding with the stem-cell transplant.

By this time, I was anxious and desperate to begin the next phase of my journey, but the hospital decided to exercise caution and patience.

"Let's see how far the COVID numbers drop," they kept saying. "Let's see." And when January came to an end, they said, "Let's see how February looks."

So, I waited, and every day I did. I went to a book of the Bible, Psalm 23:4, a place where I had begun to draw faith, strength, and courage, and prayed the words: "Even though I walk through the darkest valley, I will fear no evil, for you are with me." I said these words so much they became a mantra, a food for my soul.

I also found solitude in silence, too, and in my silence, I spun words and thoughts around in my mind. I thought about how people often said what doesn't kill you makes you stronger, and I realized those words were not a hundred percent true. Some people became stronger after experiencing terrible, horrible events, but only if they were strong to begin with.

Some people crumbled under the weight of their trauma, and I wondered if I would be one of those people. I'd always thought of myself as strong and resilient, and the past few months had proven that to me, but it had also shown me how easily I could have broken down—had I not had the love and support of friends and family. What makes you stronger isn't the thing that almost kills you; it's the people who are around to pick you back up when you fall. It's the God who loves you ever so dearly.

By the time my transplant came around, I knew I had all the strength I would ever need, not only because I was strong but because I had people who would be strong for and with me.

A week before my stem-cell transplant, I went through a psychological evaluation to see how mentally ready I was. I was as ready as I would ever be.

A night before my transplant, restless and unable to sleep, I grabbed my phone for some mindless scrolling, and I stumbled on an aging app. By simply capturing a photo of me now, it would show me what I would look like in twenty years. I took a photo and waited patiently for the results to load. When it did, it felt like I was staring into the face of my Dad. I cried then; I hadn't realized how much I'd missed him.

On the day of my transplant, knowing we were about to spend approximately twelve days in a controlled environment, Monica and I packed all that we would need: a change of clothes, entertainment, and essentials. Due to the Methodist Hospital COVID protocols, we would not be able to leave the room. The stem-cell transplant in itself would take about thirty minutes to an hour; it was the aftermath we prepared for. We got there bright and early, and the doctors were ready for us. Monica and I were ushered into a small hospital room, one that had been totally cleaned and sterilized. As it dawned on us, we would have no physical contact with the outside world for the next two weeks. We looked at each other and held hands.

"This is sort of like a camping trip deep in the woods," I said.

"Totally," Monica said. "Except it's a hospital."

I chuckled. We were about to face one of life's biggest challenges—death; a little humor was certainly needed. I distracted myself by looking around and marveled at how much equipment the hospital had fit into 150 square feet of space.

My doctors, Dr. Alvarenga and Dr. Cruz were direct opposites of each other. Dr. Alvarenga was serious and stern, while Dr. Cruz had a quirky and friendly bedside manner. Ironically, because his appearance still reminded me of an admiral. I appreciated having both personalities attend to me. It felt balanced somehow.

To begin, they flooded my body with a high dosage of Melphalan to kill off my immune system. Afterward, I was to wait twenty-four hours before my stem cells could be reapplied to my body. Those twenty-four hours were some of the hardest of my life. As I sat there, completely stripped of all my defenses, my mind spun with all the things that could go wrong. What if the room hadn't been sterilized properly? What if my body caught some virus or germs from the air? How many other people had used this room before me? Had they all made it out alive? They showed me my numbers, and it seemed impossible that I was still alive. My stem cell count was incredibly low. Once again, I marveled at modern medicine.

Before I went in, Monica had texted my daughters and my mom, and to distract myself, I asked if any of them had reached out.

"Just Victoria and Mom," she said.

"And Gabriela?" I asked hopefully.

She shook her head sadly. "She will come around someday, Mi Amor. Just focus on getting better again."

Monica was right; I needed to focus on getting better. I couldn't repair my relationship with my daughter if I were dead. I hoped she would come around someday because I intended to put in the work to fight to repair our relationship, just as I was fighting to live now.

After the twenty-four hours were up, my rebirth began.

Day zero started around mid-morning with a flurry of nurses, doctors, and staff entering my room, bringing in an additional table, a large cryogenic tank that contained my frozen stem cells, and one tabletop heater. I watched as the staff began the process: my frozen stem cells were pulled from the tank, and the numbers that were collected during my stem-cell collection were verified and validated by two separate medical staff personnel.

"What number of stem cells would be placed back into my body?" I asked

"Four million," one of the head nurses answered.

"That many?" I asked. I recalled the magic number being approximately two million, three at the most. Not four million.

"Don't worry, Mr. Proctor," she said. "We've got this."

But I was worried. What would happen to me if they exceeded the quantity of stem cells? I watched as the nurse placed the frozen stem cells into a tabletop heater and warmed them up so they could be extracted from the bag and placed into a large syringe. The participating nursing staff warned Monica and me that the smell would be strong and have the scent of tomato sauce.

True to her words, the powerful smell of tomato sauce filled the room, and I found myself thinking it was such an inappropriate time to think of pasta. Then, I found myself wondering if I would ever eat pasta again. The injection of my stem cells into my body took approximately twenty-five minutes, and I began the start of my eleven-day incubation period. As I dozed off, I found myself, strangely, dreaming of pasta.

Day +1

I have no memory. Monica says I slept like the dead. "You were completely out!" she said. "If the doctors hadn't told me it was normal, I would have been so worried. Your mom called, too. She wanted to talk, but I told her you were out."

Day +2

More sleep. I came in and out of consciousness, barely aware of my surroundings. It felt like my body wasn't mine, like I was out of it, trying to make my way back. Monica told me more people called. "Robert and Jackie," she said. "Kalee, too. They were very concerned and encouraging. Somehow—and I don't know how—Kalee was able to get us that water you like. You know how impossible it's been to get during this COVID shortage. Kalee's really something!"

I smiled. Kalee was something. I'd known her for years professionally, but her soft and caring nature morphed our relationship into a friendship. I wasn't surprised about the water. This was the sort of thing she would do. Kalee was very resourceful.

Day +3

My body slowly started to make its way out of hibernation, and I came out of the blur of my mind to a ravishing thirst. My body was completely dehydrated, and like a man stuck in a scorching desert, I yearned for water. The doctors immediately put me on a one-liter IV to get my water levels back up. I went back to sleep with the image of Monica's face—etched with worry—in my mind.

When I woke up, immensely grateful for it, I drank the water Kalee had graciously coordinated and sent to us in the hospital.

Day +4

I started to feel a little like myself again. I was more alert when the doctors came in to ask questions and when the cool, detached nurse took my vitals. Monica didn't look as worried, and to pass the time, she read all the messages that had come in while I was under, or as she called it, in a medical coma.

Day +5

I woke up to the lyrics of "Man in the Mirror," a Michael Jackson song, playing in the background. For the first time, I listened to the lyrics closely and felt an awakening, a surge to do something different, something good that day. It didn't matter that I was lying on my hospital bed, still very much unable to walk.

I struck up a conversation with the detached nurse when she came in to check my vitals, and it turned out she was quite friendly when she wanted to be and had a very beautiful smile. Her name was Paige. She worked the night shift and provided us with extensive care to ensure that everything was going smoothly for us. From our first day in the hospital, she ensured all things were in order for both Monica and me. She had, unknown to us, asked the hospital dietitian to schedule meals for Monica, knowing she would be unable to leave the room, too. The more we talked to her, the more grateful we were for her bedside professionalism and attention to detail. Over the days of getting to know each other better, we shared with her things that we had going on in our lives and talked about how the diagnosis had flipped our world upside down.

One day, as she checked my vitals, I asked, "Would you like to come on our podcast sometime?"

"Sounds interesting," she said. "I'll listen and let you know."

Day +6

I tried to read a book but put it down after a few pages because I was too groggy. I asked Monica if Gabriela had called, but she said *no*. I went back to reading my book and fell asleep shortly afterward.

Day +7

I started to feel claustrophobic in the tiny hospital room and decided to move around. But there was nowhere to walk to, and even if I wanted to, my body was too weak to move except for a few paces. The doctors advised me to rest. "You'll have plenty of time to move around," they said. "Let your body heal."

Day +8

Feeling down, anxious, and closed in, I read the words of Psalms 23 again. I was reminded that God was always willing to meet us in our brokenness and pain. I was eager to get to the other side of this transplant, but I had no idea what was on the other side of it except God. He was always at the beginning, middle, and end of everything. I read those words over and over, and on day eight, they brought me immeasurable comfort.

Day +9

I woke up with uncontrollable shivering. My insides felt cold, and my fingers were numb. I couldn't move, and my vision was a blurry mess. An hour later, I experienced intense diarrhea. The sickness was made even more horrifying and embarrassing because I couldn't make my way quickly to the bathroom. Monica yelled for the doctors and held me as I shivered. After what seemed like forever but was actually a few minutes, they came in, gave me some steroids to control the shivering and diarrhea, and I sank into a deep sleep.

The first question I asked when I woke up was, "What was that? I thought I was getting better."

"You are," my doctors said. "But what you experienced was engraftment syndrome, and that's normal for a transplant patient. The thing about a stem-cell transplant is when your cells are injected back into your body. They have no idea what they are or where to go. The nausea, vomiting, aches, and fever are them trying to figure that out. It's as if your own body is in a war with you like it's been attacked."

"But you are through the worst of it now," they said. "Everything should be fine from here on out."

As the days wore on, my body continued to adapt. The hours began to seem particularly long, and by Day +10, Monica and I began to get antsy being stuck in the room. My doctors still came in every few hours to check my vitals and make sure everything was progressing accordingly. One part that really fascinated me was my heartbeat. Before we got into the hospital, it was seventy to eighty beats per minute. During the incubation period, it fluctuated, going up and down, up and down. I would be sitting down, and my heart would be racing a mile a minute.

The more they came to check on me, the more frequently we asked if it was okay for us to go home.

"Not yet," Nurse Paige would say. Or, "You asked that an hour ago." Or, and my least favorite, "You've still got several more days, Mr. Proctor."

So, it surprised me when Dr. Cruz and Dr. Alvarenga came in on Day +11 and asked, "Mr. Proctor, would you like to go home?"

"Yes," I said immediately.

And they both laughed. I was grateful to be feeling much better, but I really was losing my mind being there.

"Is it safe for us to leave?" Monica asked.

Dr. Cruz consulted his notes. "So far, his vitals are stable, and he's being receptive to food and the drinks and the drugs. His symptoms are not out of the ordinary. I think it's safe to say you can go home."

I smiled even wider.

"But please, you need to be careful," Dr. Alvarenga added. "Keep Mr. Proctor isolated and clean. He is still at risk."

"Of course," Monica said, smiling just as much as I was. "Absolutely."

And so the next day, we packed our bags and went home, unaware of what was to come. Later on, I would think that we would have avoided all that came next if we had made the decision to stay one more day.

Fourteen hours after we got home, I spiked a horrible fever.

It started out slow and non-threatening. My skin was a little warm at first, so we didn't think much of it. But all of a sudden, the fever spiked, and my body hurt so bad I felt like I was going to die. In a panic, Monica broke most of our safety rules and drove me to the hospital. The doctors took one look at me and admitted me back into the isolated emergency room. An hour later, my fever spiked again and reached heights the doctors had never encountered before. In fear and panic, Monica paced and cried and asked the only question that made sense to her at the time, "What is wrong with him? Is it engraftment syndrome? Is that it?"

The doctors shook their heads in confusion and proceeded to run every test on me: bloodwork, ultrasound, X-rays, EKG, major organs functional test, erythrocyte sedimentation rate, urinalysis, and basic cultures. All of them came back negative.

"Well, what is it?!" Monica cried.

"We don't know, Mrs. Proctor."

"Why not? We barely spent a few hours at home."

"Well, tell us what happened when you left here. When you left the hospital, where did you go?"

"We went straight home," Monica sobbed. "No, no, we went to a drive-through first. But he was inside the car the entire time, and he never took off his mask."

"What did he eat?"

"Uhm, uh, just some rice and chicken, but he barely ate it. He was too weak."

"Could it be sepsis?" some of the attending ER doctors mentioned.

"Sepsis?!" Monica exclaimed. "His immune system can't take that. He'll die!"

So, they ran more and more tests, bringing in more and more doctors, checking for bacteria and other viral infections—all of which came back negative. I developed a skin rash on the third day, and by the sixth day, the doctors decided that it had to be one thing— engraftment syndrome. The very thing Monica had suggested on the first day.

"It's very common in patients who have just undergone a bone marrow transplant,' they said. "But your husband will be fine."

My fever broke on the seventh day, and on the eighth day, I went home with my wife.

My rebirth had been much harder than I'd expected, not that I expected it to be easy. But those seven days where they poked and prodded but couldn't find anything wrong with me had terrified me.

I had thought after remission, after the transplant, after months of treatment and growth and clarity, that I was going to die. But in those moments of fear, weakness, and uncertainty, my faith, strength, and courage anchored me.

I'm not saying I'm responsible for my life—God is. I'm just saying I was very determined not to die.

Gregory 2.0

You don't realize how meaningful days are until you are at a point where you have to count them, where every second becomes a precious, priceless thing that you cannot do without. It had been 242 days since my diagnosis, 150 days since I went into remission, 57 days since my stem cells were collected, and 37 days since my transplant. Some days had been excruciating; others had been terrifying; some had been good, others bad. But all of them had been priceless, tangible, and valuable because, from the moment I was diagnosed, my life stopped being routine and became a race for survival, morphing eventually into gratitude. And on the day I walked out of that hospital room alive, I knew the old Gregory had died in there, and the new one had been given a second chance.

Days after we came home, my mom visited to help and support my recovery. She had monitored my transplant from her apartment through calls and, with all the attention of a new mom, fixated on the baby monitor while her baby slept. This was fitting because my immune system was like that of a baby: fragile, an infectious sneeze away from crumbling. I had to be isolated, so when my mom visited, she sat several feet away and watched me sleep, smiling when I woke up and noticed her, looking at me like she couldn't believe I had made it out but not doubting for a second that I would. She had tears in her eyes the first time she saw me, and I wanted to forget all the health protocols, go over them, and hug her.

With her around, Monica got a breather. My mom insisted on helping with cooking, cleaning, running errands, and whatever else we needed. Monica followed her around, insisting she could handle everything, but my mom insisted even harder.

"You rest, dear," she said. "You deserve as much rest as Gregory."

To celebrate the success of my recovery, she made her famous pound cake. Of course, I couldn't eat anything that sugary, but it was such a treat for Monica.

Being alive and well felt so new, so good, so exhilarating, and I didn't want to waste a minute of it. I wanted to get up and get going, to put into motion this new life I'd been given, to enjoy every second, every step of it. I wanted the world to know that I was back and I'd made it to the other side.

But I paced myself, determined to stop and breathe and really soak in my recovery. It was as if God was saying, "Rest, I have so much for you to do. Don't be in a hurry. There's plenty of work up ahead." So, with that in mind, I spent my recovery in appreciation, reaching out to people who had checked in on me.

My siblings called every day to make sure my transplant was going well. They stayed in touch with Monica through the journey, finally breathing a sigh of relief when I came home.

Robert, who had monitored my transplant like a hawk. When I returned, he sent me tips to aid my recovery and jokes to make me laugh. I talked to him a lot while I was in isolation and a lot more as I came out of it.

"What's next?" he asked. "What's next for Gregory 2.0?"

I honestly didn't know yet. But I knew no one besides God knew how important it was for me to live, and I was not about to take that for granted.

Victoria called and reassured me, loving and supporting me enough for her and her sister. I didn't know if Gabriela would reach out. I didn't know if she would ever want to rekindle our relationship, but I was thankful for Victoria. And though I constantly prayed that my Gabriela would come around, for now, Victoria was more than enough.

Kalee who called regularly after my recovery to ask how else she could help. I'd laughed gratefully and told her everything was going well. "Okay," she'd said, laughing too. "Let me know if you need more bottles of water."

Jackie, who was quick to remind me that she told me all would be well. "I knew you would make it," she said in delight. "I told you God would take care of it."

Monica watched my blood pressure and oxygen numbers and checked my vitals daily. "Everything still looks good," she said with a smile after each check. "Very good."

While we both knew that I was very far from engaging with the real world because my immune system was still fragile, there was no denying that I was back.

I began my post-transplant check-ups a week after returning home. While I understood these follow-up procedures were important to keep my cancer at bay, going to them made me anxious. The biopsy, though bearable, didn't get less painful. But every time I thought about that or some part of me even tried to whine, I reminded myself that a year ago, I didn't even think I would be here. Not only had I survived, but I came out with redirected motivation and renewed inspiration. I'd become a person with every intention of living every single moment to the fullest. I thought that was who I had always been, but battling and recovering from cancer showed me I'd been on autopilot all my life. I had learned lessons, lessons that would stay with me forever, and now all I wanted was to share these lessons with others, to bring them from a place of despair into hope and inspiration.

This purpose became all the more glaring when Monica and I were walking the trails. We were up to thirty-six miles a week by then. We had started with ten miles per week.

That day, as we walked away from the noisiness of everyday life into the quietness of nature, we saw a few deer— shy, beautiful creatures that hid or leaped out of the way when they heard noises or saw people. It made me chuckle how they hid away from us, from a place that was more theirs than ours. But I guess humans are like that sometimes; we hide away from things and places we should take charge of.

As we walked on, we came across an exquisite kaleidoscope of black butterflies. They had red and tiny white spots on the edges of their wings and flew with such gentleness and grace. Monica and I paused and stared in awe as they glided over our heads. It was such a beautiful moment, and I held her hands as they did. When we got home, I headed straight for my laptop and typed in the words—black butterflies. That moment had felt symbolic, and I knew it had to mean something.

According to my search results, in many cultures, black butterflies were considered a symbol of misfortune and death. While in other cultures, it was a symbol of positive change, a sign of renewal, rebirth, and transition.

I thought about how I felt standing under them as they flew over Monica and me, how their wings fluttered so gently, how their very aura instilled peace, and I wondered how anyone could see something so beautiful and think of death or misfortune. But then I realized that signs don't come with meanings; it's humans who assign meaning to them. To me, this butterfly meant life. It meant the meaning of every situation wasn't found in the beginning but in the journey and resolution. Signs and life were what you made of them.

Filled with inspiration, I closed my laptop and walked to the bathroom to take a shower. Monica and I had a blood cancer live-stream fundraiser to attend. It was titled: Open Your Hearts and Wallets for Blood Cancer.

All cancer patients share a fear that their cancer will come back. For some, that fear is fitful; for others, it's constant. They walk around with it, fearing the next biopsy will reveal the thing they dread. For me, this fear was fitful, and it coupled with the knowledge that no male in my family had lived past sixty-five years. While I believed I was healed, while I believed God had taken me through this journey and out of my cancer, I still worried a little when I went for a biopsy result. I wondered what it would say, and I always hoped for a negative.

For my third biopsy after the transplant, Monica and I sat in the transplant lobby waiting to see our transplant doctor. It was eighty-seven days after my transplant and two weeks after my last biopsy. Of course, the last two were negative, and we were anxious to get a third. I looked over at Monica as she sat, tapping her feet anxiously. She was just as anxious as I was, maybe even more. I tried not to think about the horror of having the result come back positive. I didn't even want to imagine it. It would be fine, I told myself repeatedly. You've made it to the other side, Gregory. You will be fine.

"Are you nervous?" Monica asked.

"Me?" I said with mock nonchalance. "Whatever for?"

She laughed, and that eased some of my worry. "It's going to be fine," she said.

"Absolutely," I replied.

We waited another fifteen minutes before a nurse came over to tell us apologetically that we couldn't speak to our transplant doctor today.

"He's not in," she said.

Monica and I looked at her in surprise. How could he not be in? "We are scheduled to meet him today," I said. "It's been two weeks since my test. The results should be out by now."

"I'm sorry," the nurse replied.

"Can we speak to a head nurse? Or a manager?" Monica asked.

"When can we get the result if we don't get it today?" I added.

"Two weeks from now."

"No," I said. The thought of waiting another two weeks to find out if my cancer was back or gone unnerved me. I was just getting back to myself, feeling and doing good. The not-knowing would send me spiraling.

"Why exactly can't we speak to our doctor today?" I asked.

The nurse spoke sheepishly, "The coordinating nurse failed to order the additional lab blood work."

"Why not?"

"A simple mix-up. These things unfortunately happen."

"So how long do we have to wait for this to be clarified?"

"Two weeks."

"No."

Monica pulled me aside. "She doesn't know much, Mi Amor. I suggest we find a coordinator or a manager and get this sorted out."

So, we did. We thanked the nurse, waited for her to walk away, and went in search of the coordinator. When we found her, she looked harried and overwhelmed. I could see immediately why she had forgotten to send the blood work.

Monica approached her, and I watched from a small distance as they conversed in low tones. A few minutes later, Monica smiled, and I knew we were going to get the results today. The coordinator took us to a different doctor, drew labs, and I even received my Evusheld shots. Since my transplant, I'd been given a vaccine schedule to retake the important flu and vaccine shots I'd taken years before. After another hour of waiting, we got the biopsy results back. It was negative.

I didn't realize how much I'd been holding my breath until I read the results. Monica hugged me with a radiant smile, and I knew she had been holding her breath, too. We drove back home euphoric. I thought about how people often said patience was a virtue. It was. But sometimes, impatience gets the job done. I could have spent the next fourteen days twisting my thumbs and waiting for my results. But now, I was going home with the knowledge that my cancer was at bay.

From that moment, it became all about keeping cancer in remission. And when people asked me what that was like, what it was like working and praying my cancer didn't come back, I told them it was a combination of three things:

The first was like climbing the steep trails of an amusement ride while on drugs. Except there was nothing amusing about it. I'd say, imagine you are locked into the stationary chair of a roller-coaster, and just before the ride begins, a nurse approaches you, tells the ride to halt, and proceeds to pump you full of drugs. While she inserts the needle into your chest, even though you have been through the pain many times, you are still not quite used to it, so you flinch. After that, with a calm, reassuring smile, she starts you on pre-med drugs for the nausea you are about to experience. A drug that will take about an hour to get into your system through the IV. All this happens while the ride is still waiting; it's still not begun. While the IV is running, she injects the back of your arm muscle with an Xgeva shot. You are used to the burn and stick from this shot by now, so you don't flinch as much.

It's at this point the ride begins. You are hanging on for dear life, with the drugs swirling in your system and your body pitched at a 45-degree angle, while you are looking at a full-speed, 500-foot drop. Just as the nurse injects Darzalex into your bloodstream, the brake releases, and the car drops. The drug travels through your bloodstream, and as you drop, you struggle to fight the wave of its effect. Finally, you succumb to its power, and when you come four hours later, there's a fog hanging over your head, your legs are rubber, and you have no idea where you are.

The second part is believing—believing this 500-foot drop is worth it. Believing your body is accepting the drugs. Calibrating your mind to stay positive, to keep the doubts and fears out. Half of surviving cancer is drugs; the other half is believing that you will survive it, going into it with faith, strength, and courage.

And the third? The third is God.

We spent that week on the trails again, walking and talking and taking in nature. My chemo and transplant still felt like a miracle to me. This thing I survived when I didn't think I would. Excelling at physical therapy was another way for me to be grateful, to show that I was not going to take my second chance lying down.

The cancer returned two months after the stem cell transplant.

Not mine, my friend Robert Allen. Allen and I, as I came to call him to differentiate from my other friend Robert, met nine weeks prior to our scheduled stem-cell transplant while sitting in the lobby of the Methodist Hospital Blood Cancer & Stem Cell Transplant Clinic, waiting to be called back for our consultation visit. At the time, we didn't know we were both scheduled to see Dr. Cruz. We'd simply locked eyes and smiled, and I liked Allen immediately. He had an aura that was inviting, positive, and friendly.

To pass the time, we started a conversation, and I mentioned I had multiple myeloma and Dr. Cruz was my transplant doctor.

"Wow!" he exclaimed. "I have MM, too, and Dr. Cruz is also my doctor. When are you scheduled to have your transplant?"

"I'm targeting the third week of January 2022. But that really depends on the COVID numbers."

"Yeah." He sighed sadly. "COVID."

We spent the rest of our time in the lobby getting acquainted with each other and discussing what each of us did for work and for fun. The more we talked, the more I liked him. I liked it even more that he shared the same name with one of my dearest friends.

"I have a podcast, you know," I said, and Monica chuckled, probably because, as she'd said, I sounded like an excited little boy every time I mentioned it. I couldn't help it. My podcast really gave me joy.

"No kidding," Allen said. "I'm looking to start mine soon."

We laughed over the coincidence and continued talking about our diagnosis and how it changed our lives. As we walked off to our respective examining rooms, we promised to keep in touch.

"Definitely," Allen said as he shook my hand. "We are transplant brothers now."

From that day, we maintained contact with each other right up until the day we both got admitted into the hospital for our transplant. Allen was released one day before me during my original eleven days, prior to being readmitted back into the hospital for engraftment syndrome. After that, Allen and I sort of lost touch.

I had gotten so occupied with my post-transplant check-ups and vaccination schedules that I'd forgotten to reach out. But after my third biopsy came back negative, I reached out to Allen, hoping we could share this too. Over the phone, I happily gave my update and asked about his. But he went horribly quiet.

"Allen?" I asked.

"It's back," he said. "Mine's back."

Too stunned to speak, I remained silent. The silence between us stretched, and I recognized it. It was the same one my friends and family had when I first gave them my news.

"I just want to be done, Greg," Allen said. "I'm tired, and I want to be done."

After I ended the call with Allen, I stayed in bed and cried. And a few days later, still depressed from the news, I realized I was suffering from survivor's guilt. Here I was, healthy and in remission, while my friend was right back where we started. I felt so unworthy of my healing, so undeserving.

A few more days later, after praying and reflecting, I pulled up my email and wrote to Allen. I told him I was sorry about his result. I told him I was rooting for him. I told him he would make it out. Do you know why? I said, "Because God will take care of you, as He did me." I felt better after hitting send. I hoped Allen did when he read it, too.

On the morning of my 52nd birthday, I woke up to the most beautiful day. I looked back on the past year, my journey, and my life and realized once again it was nothing short of a miracle that I was alive. In the past six months, I have doubled my efforts to bring awareness to the multiple myeloma society, particularly the funding part, by guesting on numerous podcasts to talk about it. It's like I said on one of the LLS podcast episodes titled, LLS Financial Assistance,

How Can We Help:

"Most people won't be able to deal with these types of things. Maybe they don't have family support, or maybe they haven't thought that far in their lives, and my heart goes out to those types of folks, and that's why it's so important for me to be a part of what we're discussing today because these things are out there and it's just a matter of people having the awareness to know where to go and how to participate in these programs.

The way I see it, it's impossible to participate in these programs if you aren't aware of them. But LLS wasn't the only program I talked about. There are many opportunities for financial assistance out there. People just need to be aware of them."

I also joined the LLS team in San Antonio to raise funds, awareness, and provisions for multiple myeloma patients. My target was two million dollars. My team called it a stretch, but I was determined to raise as much as I could for the people who needed it. These people were me a year ago, and I wanted to give all the help I could.

I had also gone back to consulting but was now working only twenty hours a week. My life was more than work now; my life had more meaning.

Later that day, I checked my phone and saw I had birthday messages pouring in from everywhere. My mom, my siblings, Robert, Victoria, Kalee, and even my doctors called to wish me a happy birthday. My social media blew up with hundreds of messages, and Monica had already wished me a happy birthday at twelve a.m. with a soft kiss.

As I went through my messages, noting one from Allen, he was alive and fighting, thank God, I paused and thought about my journey, my life, my friends and family, Monica, my daughters, and my renewed faith. I was here; I had made it not because of anything special I had done; I made it because God decided so.

Not only had I made it, but my journey had reshaped my life and taught me how to see the best in the worst. I've learned to measure days in relationships, fortitude, and grace rather than time, productivity, or work. I've been taught by some of the weakest and sickest about courage, determination, and strength. I don't always live in this newly discovered ground, but I'm always aware of its invitation, each moment becoming another chance to try again, to choose differently. And more than anything, I wished that for Allen.

Filled with gratitude, I dropped my phone, blended up a fruit smoothie, and went out onto the patio. The air was crisp, and the morning was calm. While I sat there on the patio, I reflected upon how faith, strength, and courage are often considered to be interconnected concepts that can help individuals persevere through difficult times.

Faith is a belief or trust in something or someone, often related to spiritual or religious beliefs. It can provide individuals with a sense of purpose and comfort and can help them navigate challenges with a sense of hope and optimism. In my case, this faith was God.

Strength can refer to both physical and mental resilience. Physical strength can help individuals overcome physical challenges, while mental strength can help them cope with emotional difficulties and stress. Building strength can involve pushing through discomfort or difficulty to achieve a goal or overcome obstacles. In my case, my strength was bolstered by my friends and family.

Courage is the ability to face fear, danger, or adversity with bravery and determination. It requires individuals to step outside their comfort zones and take risks, even when they are uncertain about the outcome. I'd always stepped outside my comfort zone and always had courage. With my cancer, I just had to channel it differently.

Together, faith, strength, and courage can provide individuals with a sense of purpose, resilience, and determination that can help them overcome challenges and achieve their goals.

I took a deep breath and felt a rush of gratitude flow through me. I knew none of this at fifty, understood it at fifty-one, and now, at fifty-two, it had become a certainty.

I didn't know what lessons fifty-two held for me, but I knew whatever happened, however, it went, it would be amazing.

Financial Aid and Transportation Programs for Multiple Myeloma and Other Blood Cancers

1. Leukemia & Lymphoma Society

CO-PAY ASSISTANCE PROGRAM

Contact Us: (877) 557-2672 | FinancialAssistance@lls.org

Website: https://www.lls.org/support-resources/financial-support/co-pay-assistance-program

2. Patient Advocate Foundation

Co-Pay Relief

Website: https://copays.org/funds/multiple-myeloma/

3. Amgen Assist 360

Drug: Xgeva

Website: https://www.amgensupportplus.com/copay?referID=AA360

4. Janssen Prescription Assistance

Drug: Darzalex

Contact Us: 844-55DARZA (844-553-2792)

Website:
https://www.janssencarepath.com/patient/darzalex/patient-support

5. Takeda Oncology

Drug: Velcade

Contact Us: 1-844-817-6468, Option 2

Website: https://www.here2assist.com/patient/home

6. Mercy Medical Angels

Transportation: Flights for Veterans

Contact Us 888.675.1405

Website: www.MercyMedical.org

7. San Antonio Coalition for Veterans and Families

Veteran Support & Community Resources

Contact Us: (210) 990-1115

Website: https://sacvf.org/

Educational Programs for Multiple Myeloma Patients and Other Blood Cancers

1.   HealthTree Foundation

Website: https://healthtree.org/

2.   The Multiple Myeloma Research Foundation (MMRF)

Website: https://themmrf.org/

3.   International Myeloma Foundation (IMF)

Website: https://www.myeloma.org/

4.   National Bone Marrow Transplant Link (NBMT Link)

Website: https://www.nbmtlink.org/

5.   The National Comprehensive Cancer Network (NCCN)

Website: https://www.nccn.org/home

6. Leukemia & Lymphoma Society

Website: https://lls.org/myeloma/myeloma-overview

About the Author

Gregory O. Proctor is a distinguished survivor, advocate, and author who has faced and triumphed over the challenges of multiple myeloma. Diagnosed amidst the tumultuous backdrop of the COVID-19 pandemic, Gregory navigated the complexities of the healthcare system with tenacity and determination. While the uncertainties of his condition and global events could have deterred many, Gregory's steadfast spirit and profound faith transformed him into an emblem of hope for many in similar straits.

Guided by his journey, Gregory offers his narrative with candid vulnerability, recognizing the power of his experiences to embolden others. He emphasizes the vital role of mindset in recovery, attributing his own healing to a positive attitude and a concentrated presence in each moment. Bolstered by an unwavering faith and the steadfast support of his loved ones, he has weathered many challenges, continuously finding strength in adversity.

As an advocate in the realm of multiple myeloma, Gregory's contributions have been pivotal. Working alongside esteemed organizations such as the Leukemia & Lymphoma Society, he has been a catalyst for raising awareness and facilitating research funding. His advocacy not only champions the cause but also extends hope and support to countless individuals and families affected by the disease.

Throughout his journey with cancer, Gregory has unearthed numerous lessons and unexpected blessings. The bonds forged, the lives impacted, and the ability to instill hope stand as a testament to the positive facets of his experience. Gregory O. Proctor's unyielding drive, coupled with his radiant positivity, continues to inspire and resonate, leaving a lasting legacy. His singular perspective on cancer as an "opportunity" underlines his enduring belief in the possibility of purpose and impact, even amid adversity.